Marxist perspectives in the sociology of education

Marxist perspectives in the sociology of education

Maurice Levitas

Department of Education
Neville's Cross College of Education

ROUTLEDGE & KEGAN PAUL
London and Boston

First published in 1974
by Routledge & Kegan Paul Ltd
Broadway House, 68-74 Carter Lane,
London EC4V 5EL and
9 Park Street,
Boston, Mass. 02108, USA

Set in 10/12pt Times New Roman
and printed in Great Britain by
John Sherratt & Son Ltd
St Ann's Press, Park Road, Altrincham, Cheshire
WA14 5QQ

ISBN O 7100 7896 X
Library of Congress Catalog Card No. 74–77197

Contents

Preface

At no time has there been so widespread an interest in Marxism as during this decade. Sociologists everywhere acknowledge its importance and it would be hard to find a social issue of importance where Marxist thought is irrelevant. Education is no exception. It inspires sustained activity in teachers' organisations, in educational practice and in political pressure for a range of working class children's interests. In addition, it has provided new insights into education's history and into educational psychology.

There has been, however, no thoroughgoing application of Marxist thought to the sociology of education. This deficiency is due in part to the character of Colleges of Education where this element of educational theory has had its main reason for growth and in part to an assumption that what is of value in Marxism is incorporated in the existing literature.

But another explanation is that Marxists have welcomed support from sociology in the debate with the intelligence testers and have neglected to counter support for selection from apparent allies. It is for this reason that the major theories explored in the book are those explaining social mobility and those which derive from a relativist position in sociology. The first inform us that the easier it is for working class children to achieve high status, the more democratic is the education system; the second would persuade us of the need to tailor education to fit children for living in their various communities. These two conceptual frameworks come together in the proposition that education is primarily a distributor of life chances in a stratified society.

Exploitation more accurately defines the social relationship upon which rests the division of society into classes. The educational implications of this relationship, therefore, are what require sociological analysis. But exploitation, when it is understood by the proletariat, impels that class to strive for a classless society. In that effort goals are created which have nothing to do with social climbing. They converge in the universalistic demand for social revolution wherein education is an essential process of enlightenment and enablement.

With this orientation the book attempts five purposes: to define some key areas in the sociology of education; to give access to some important concepts of Marx and Engels; to strengthen sociological starting points by adding to them a Marxist element; to discriminate between radically different directions in education; to map the main features of an educational endeavour true to working-class long-term objectives. The intention is thus to provide a compass by which place and direction in the sociology of education can be discovered by teachers, students and parents.

My many thanks are due to Joyce Fitton for her comments on the readability of final drafts. For any mistakes, inconsistencies, and other faults, only I am to blame.

ML

Chapter 1

Marxism and the culture concept

Culture and socialisation

In 1846 in *The German Ideology* Karl Marx and Friedrich Engels wrote as follows (1938 edn, p.14):

> we do not set out from what men say, imagine, conceive, nor from men as narrated, thought of, imagined, conceived, in order to arrive at men in the flesh. We set out from real, active men and on the basis of their real life process we demonstrate the development of the ideological reflexes and echoes of this life process.

In 1859 this way of looking at human beings was expressed in a more developed way by Marx in the *Introduction to a Critique of Political Economy*: 'It is not the consciousness of men that determines their existence, but, on the contrary, their social existence determines their consciousness' (1918 edn, p.12).

The success of that theory and its pervasiveness in present day thought is expressed in the enormous importance attached to the culture concept in modern sociological thought. For social existence exactly states what anthropologists and sociologists mean when they talk about culture. And that its determining influence on the consciousness of men is not left to chance may be seen in the study of child upbringing in any society.

Because we often refer to education in its wider sense of all the pressures upon a child to understand his environment in the way adults understand it, the culture concept is a topic of primary importance in the sociology of education. This means of course that schools and teachers are not the only educators but that parents, older siblings, other relatives, neighbours, other children, the houses they live in, the things they see and touch, the sounds they hear—all social beings and social products—make up the experience of the child. These are the forces and influences to which he has to adapt, these are the forces and influences he has to learn to use for his own purposes. And his purposes express both assimilation of and accommodation to the social context within which he interacts with others. These ends manifest the meanings he derives from his environment, meanings continually tested in his experience with people and with things. A meaning is seen to be valid if it is shared—if the inference drawn from an action, a gesture, a word, a response is what is implied by the actor, speaker, respondent.

To become educated in this total way means to be socialised and it would be better to retain the term socialisation for this all-in process. Socialisation is not something peculiar to a child and it is not a process which is complete once adulthood is attained. A child is a child member of society, although, no doubt, there is a comparatively short period when an infant may be regarded as an asocial being: accorded responses by those who have anything to do with him, but, as yet, on his own part, not sharing a significant proportion of their meanings.

Children of three—or even less—rapidly reach a stage where they understand that there are meanings shared among adults in respect of children, that they themselves share meanings concerning adults, and that they share meanings about childhood with adult members of society. But childhood is not the same in every society. It differs from one culture to another, and even within a culture there can be different modes of childhood. Nothing illustrates this better than the different attitudes towards childhood in the nineteenth century. The Latey Report explains that during the last century offspring of the propertied classes were accorded childhood status up to twenty-one as a protective device against a variety of swindlers. Marx, on the other hand, discussing the Factory Act of 1833, had this to say (1926 edn, p.307):

> capital now began a noisy agitation that went on for several years. It turned chiefly on the age of those who under the name of children, were limited to eight hours of work and were subject to a certain amount of compulsory education. According to capitalist anthropology the age of childhood ended at ten or at the most at eleven. . . . They managed in fact to intimidate the

government . . . to lower the limit of the age of childhood from thirteen to twelve.

That socialisation during which a child learns to be a child becomes the process whereby he learns to be an adolescent and, eventually, to to be an adult. Socialisation then continues during every stage of adulthood into old age and ceases only in death. Even then, that there are ways of dying which are culturally apt is commonly accepted. Socialisation works because currently shared meanings are proven over and over again and because the new meanings that are learnt as life goes on, are appropriate. This is not only true of a society like ours where change is so rapid, it is true also of slowly changing societies. The reason for this is that in any society, its members, in their interaction with each other, have to reach a basis of stable expectation from day to day. That stability depends upon the same expectations being constantly realised despite changes in personnel.

Socialisation itself, as a process, depends ultimately upon the nature of mankind as a species. At whatever society we look, pre-literate, feudal, slave, industrial, the same process will be observed to be in force. What will be different will be the content of that process. Every child in every society has to learn from adults the meanings given to life by his society; but every society possesses, with a greater or lesser degree of difference, meanings to be learned. In short, every society has a culture to be learned though cultures are different.

Culture and nature

Culture is a natural product and yet there is a difference in quality between nature and culture, which has to be investigated. Claude Lévi-Strauss, in *Elementary Structures of Kinship* (1968) develops the view that whatever can be found to be variable in human life is of culture, whereas whatever can be found to be universal is of nature. Further, what characterises culture is that it is a world of rules (p.8).

> wherever there are rules we know for certain that the cultural
> stage has been reached. Likewise, it is easy to recognise
> universality as the criterion in nature, for what is constant in
> man falls necessarily beyond the scope of customs, techniques
> and institutions whereby his groups are differentiated and
> contrasted

We need not agree with Lévi-Strauss about the unique importance of the incest prohibition in the leap from nature to culture, but the definition of that leap as one 'where nature transcends itself' is highly acceptable. The union between nature and culture (p.25)

> is less a union than a transformation or a transition. Before it, culture is still non-existent; with it nature's sovereignty over man is ended. The prohibition of incest is where nature transcends itself. It sparks the formation of a new and more complex type of structure and is superimposed upon the simpler structures of physical life. . . . It brings about and is in itself the advent of a new order.

For Marxists the link between nature and culture lies less in the rules which characterise the latter than in that element of human kind which creates, defines and constantly re-defines the rules: that is, human consciousness. Thus Engels in his essay on Ludwig Feuerbach (1958 edn, p.252):

> In nature . . . there are only blind unconscious agencies acting upon one another, out of whose interplay the general law comes into operation. Nothing of all happens . . . happens as a consciously desired aim. In the history of society, on the contrary, the actors are all endowed with consciousness, are men acting with deliberation or passion, working towards definite goals; nothing happens without a conscious purpose, without an intended aim.

Nevertheless, the intentions, as well as the force and the intelligence behind them are framed by the actors' social existences, by their cultures.

Discussion on any culture takes in its ethical, aesthetic and intellectual activities besides those elements obviously social like work and kinship. It is obvious that sociology must describe and analyse all these and their inter-relationships. But two problems immediately arise: since every person must be a carrier of his own culture with its values, (i) can he arrive at 'value free' assessment of any social action or group, (ii) can he arrive at an estimate which does not in some way or other prescribe a line of action.

Now freedom arises from knowledge without which a man is in bondage, and since he cannot be omniscient he cannot be altogether free. What freedom he has therefore depends upon what knowledge he has. Knowledge, however—and therefore freedom—is recognition of what must happen, i.e. of necessity. What follows from this is that the degree of value freedom we can achieve depends upon the extent of our knowledge of the values we hold, and of those pressures demanding that we hold them. Second, no analysis of a culture is sufficient if it does not take into account its necessary constant change. In that it must show what is dying and what is emergent. But social trends are realised through striving for goals, goals which embody current value priorities.

It follows that a combination of the utmost value freedom and the fullest analysis amounts to a knowledge of those trends which are withering or which are flourishing. Prescription is inherent in the prognosis and, if knowledge can be tested for truth only in practice, commitment does not impair the scientific quality of the action advised and assisted.

Culture has been defined as a total way of life. Not the total way of life of an individual, or a type of individual, but the whole way of life of an entire society is embraced by this term. In the sociology of education great importance is placed on the culture concept in order to correct possible misconceptions about the so-called 'nature of the child'. The idea that children of a given nation or ethnic group or colour are, because of their descent, innately clever, dull, musical, brave, skilful, is no longer accepted. On the other hand, the idea that children are born with a given unchangeable intellectual endowment, that this endowment can be measured accurately at various stages of their lives and may be expressed as an intelligence quotient, and, moreover, that this endowment is the key factor to be seized upon in explaining the level of performance of a child in a range of activities, still commands considerable though waning support among teachers and educationists. In a sense we are returning to the old nature versus nurture argument in which the question of whether heredity or environment played the biggest part in a child's development was debated. But we are saying that environment must be reinterpreted to yield a more subtle and refined notion of the circumstances in which a child has to build his identity, and the culture more accurately expresses the kind of setting in which the process of socialisation goes on.

Just as the term environment with its connotation of mainly material elements has to give way to the term culture with its additional elements of values, beliefs, knowledge, mutual expectation, interaction within and between institutions, so the idea of fixed-at-birth propensity for action has to give way to another view. It is characteristic of human beings that their drives are unspecialised and that they are, as a consequence, capable of coping with a wide and changing range of activities. These two concepts taken together, that of a high human capacity for variation in response, and the culture concept, should help teachers to take a constructively optimistic standpoint in regard to the educability of children. This close interdependence of biologically inherited potentiality for action and culture transmission agencies responsible for the development of young human beings is expressed in the Plowden Report (DES, 1968), paragraph 23: 'For the cognitive stage to emerge, brain maturation is probably necessary though not of course sufficient. Without at least some degree of social stimulus the latent abilities may never be exercised and indeed the requisite cells may go un-developed.'

One conclusion to be derived from the importance of culture is that learning is a dominant characteristic of human behaviour. This is not to say that other animals do not learn. But the scope, depth and levels of thought that typify humans are such as to render it impossible to understand the behaviour of persons without reference to learning as an activity, to the source of that learning and its accumulation in the groups and in the societies to which they belong. The charioteer and the bus driver represent cultures as radically different as their occupational behaviours. But the possibility that they can be so different derives from a specifically human quality: the vastness of the range of possible human institutions and patterns of interaction that human beings can engage in. As Ruth Benedict observes in *Patterns of Culture* (1971 edn, p.171):

The great arc along which all possible human behaviours are distributed is far too immense, too full of contradictions for any one culture to utilise even any considerable portion of it.

People choose what to do. But choices are limited to workable alternatives arising from the conditions of life in society. Whatever the complex of expectations in a given society may be, they represent, as expectations in conscious minds, the actual modes of action and interaction as the only ways in which life is possible.

Culture and education

Another conclusion to be derived from the culture concept is that children are, and have to be, highly educable if they are to participate in and give continuity to the society in which they are destined to interact as adults. Children will learn even if what they learn is not always what their mentors would prefer them to learn.

What is transmitted to children, deliberately and unconsciously, by people, by their surroundings, by events, and what is acquired by them, is their culture. Having all become carriers of the culture of their society, they consolidate for each other, in their play and other forms of peer group interaction, that culture. Thus it follows that teaching, to be effective, must have regard for culture already acquired.

Just how important a formative force culture is, is brought out by Berger and Luckmann in *The Social Construction of Reality* (1967, p.66):

> If one looks at the matter in terms of organismic development
> it is possible to say that the foetal period in the human being
> extends through about the first year after birth. . . . At this time
> however, the human infant is not only in the outside world,
> but is interrelating with it in a number of complex ways . . .
> the developing human being not only interrelates with a
> particular natural environment but with a specific cultural and
> social order, which is mediated to him by the significant others
> who have charge of him.

There are many studies by anthropologists, easily available to us these days, of the cultures of pre-literate societies. From these one can become aware of the variety of patterns of culture which can arise on the basis of very limited technological development. Then again comparisons may be made between cultures situated in different parts of the world. It is this comparative method which makes available to us, directly, evidence concerning the variability of possible human behaviours, and reduces reliance on human nature for an explanation of how people act.

Historians make comparisons in another way. Their studies make us aware that comparisons between cultures in one region can also be made in terms of time. Thus England in 1801 with a population of about ten millions was very different from England in 1901 with a population of thirty-seven millions. But however we discover the diversity of cultures we should eventually be brought to understand that we are ourselves part of a culture and that this culture is as analysable as any other.

From this understanding should follow a realisation on the part of the teacher, that for himself, as much as for his pupils, beliefs, values, assumptions, knowledge, style of living, expectations, purposes, all form expressions of a culture which can be subjected to description and analysis. Without the application of such criticism there can be no proper understanding of what is going on in a teacher's practice.

The materialist conception of history

What Marxism adds to what has been said so far is that cultures are to be understood not only in their diversity but in the pattern of that diversity. One element in that pattern is that each culture represents a stage in social development. The experience of humanity is cumulative. The accumulations are realised in tools, weapons, techniques, which considerably affect institutional arrangements and the meanings and purposes and intentions arising therefrom. But if each culture is part of a development, development itself is of major importance. What a society is likely to become demands priority of attention. From this point of view the central enquiry is always into those forces within a culture which promote or obstruct further development.

Stages and development are associated with the idea of progress and there are not a few, who, though they cultivate the culture concept, will not admit that progress—a continuous movement towards a better order of society—is to be discerned in social development. Marxists are not alone, of course, in holding the more optimistic view, but they are probably alone in being able to account for the disfavour into which the idea of progress has fallen. Identification with progress suited the innovatory rule of the capitalist class all over Europe for well over a century. Now that capitalism is to be progressed from, the idea of progress is less comfortably held—except by those who see in the working class the makers of the next stage and commit themselves to its achievement.

That perspective insists that what has been is the source of what is to be. There are of course goals and intentions which stand opposed to inevitable change. These purposes must delay and distort progress but they must ultimately vanish as they become less and less relevant. But because Marxists direct attention to processes, and relate things, and what is immediately apparent, to processes, society and the succession of cultures and of stages are summed up in the term 'history'. Hegel's contribution to this is acknowledged by Engels in his essay on Ludwig Feuerbach, section iv and is summed up as being (1958 edn, p.248),

The great basic thought that the world is not to be comprehended as a complex of ready-made things, but as a complex of processes in which the things, apparently stable, no less than their mind-images in our heads, the concepts, go through an uninterrupted change of coming into being and passing away, in which, in spite of all seeming accidentality and of all temporary retrogression, a progressive development asserts itself in the end.

To this concept of history Marx and Engels brought a conviction that the material requirements of life determines ideas. That is, in contrast with Hegel, they had a materialist and not an idealist outlook. Thus comes into being their distinctive 'materialist conception of history'.

It is held here that this way of looking at educational institutions and problems of education in general is a necessary one for teachers whose view of professional life is not restricted to classroom interaction as it presently occurs, and whose interest extends to the force that education might exert in society as a whole. It cannot be doubted that education has progressed. Equally certain is that this progress has not been uninterrupted. A progressive development is easily discovered. As for the present, there is no dearth of issues where further progress is deemed to be urgent. And we can be sure that whatever improvements are brought into effect they will ultimately provide grounds for yet more innovation of a progressive sort. To the extent that thinking about education is related to the forces for progressive change in the wider society, to that extent will it employ, not only the culture concept but also the more inclusive and the more forward looking materialist conception of history.

Chapter 2

Social structure

The unity of subcultures

In introducing the culture concept we stressed that there are good reasons for teachers to master this idea. First, the culture concept places its emphasis upon the human being as a learning animal and therefore upon the educability of children. Second, if understanding of this concept is strengthened by analyses of cultures other than our own we may be brought to examine our own culture and therefore to know better what we are doing as teachers when we engage in its transmission and continuation. Third, if cultures are compared on a time scale, that is, if the culture of a group analysed at one time is compared with the culture of its descendant group at a later time, it will be seen that whilst continuity is inevitable a culture is not eternal. Continuity always partners change. And since cultures do change the teacher may be brought to think about what is obsolescent and what is developing—what is likely to have a greater future in our society. Fourth, since we select the kinds of knowledge, the orders of belief, the range of opinions, the variety of skills, the media of aesthetic expression to be organised into a timetable or into an integrated day of learning at school, and since all these are but elements of our culture, the culture concept is essential to a proper view of the curriculum of the schools. Any worthwhile innovatory approach to the curriculum must take into account appropriateness for a changing society and for the growing members of society, of what is to be learned or studied.

A fifth reason has to be elaborated. We start here from the principle that no individual can be familiar with the entirety of his culture. At its simplest there is always a division of labour in society no matter how elementary. This results always in some area of knowledge or some particular skill remaining outside the competence of every single member. This is so though all members of a society have meanings in common. For the sharing of meanings is contained in the division of labour whereby each can work for others and be worked for by them.

No individual can be familiar with the entirety of his culture. But there are degrees and kinds of unfamiliarity, and in a social division of labour such as we encounter in class societies, it is not a matter of individuals finding reciprocity with other individuals, though this also must take place, but of entire groups estranged from each other. In that estrangement exists a complementarity which is at the same time an antagonism. Marx and Engels in *The German Ideology* define the situation as follows (1965 edn, p.21):

These three moments, the forces of production, the state of society, and consciousness, can and must come into contradiction with one another, because the division of labour implies the possibility—nay, the fact—that intellectual and material activity—enjoyment and labour—production and consumption— devolve on different individuals and that the only possibility of their not coming into contradiction lies in the negation in its turn of the division of labour.

The difference between groups are to be seen in styles of living, stocks of ideas, modes of communication, orders of values and legal standings. But the groups are necessary integral parts of the given society. Their ways of life taken together in their interaction make up the total pattern of culture. Nevertheless the groups have their own patterns of shared meanings. To call them culture patterns, as Ralph Linton does, may cause some confusion if we are calling the overall design a pattern of culture after Ruth Benedict. But we can refer to them as subcultures as long as we remember that the prefix does not imply any inferiority. The matter is seen more clearly perhaps if we say that the subculture of the aristocracy of England in the fifteenth century was a complement of the subculture of the peasantry in the same country of the same era, and that both were, with other subcultures, necessary elements in a general pattern of culture that may be called 'feudal'. The subcultures make up the culture and yet the overall culture is more than sum of its parts: there are common meanings, means of communication and special institutions which give the culture a unity.

This unity can be expressed in yet another way. Each subculture comprising the particular series of actions by which it can be defined requires the existence of the others. Let the aristocracy begin to change its economic behaviour and to enclose arable land with a view to turning it over to sheep-rearing and the peasants who once tilled it will find themselves no longer peasants, but paupers. Let the working class succeed in their demand that the mines be nationalised, but with compensation, and the mineowners are no longer mineowners, but owners of government stock on which they draw interest.

The fifth importance that the culture concept has for the teacher comes to this then. It is that he can understand thereby that youngsters he teaches bear the culture of society in the form of subcultures: that is, they impute to the phenomena they encounter subcultural meanings. Among these phenomena which they encounter is the teacher himself whose own view of his role may or may not be the same as that of his pupils. And of course, the teacher bears, just as his pupils do, a subcultural orientation to the overall pattern of culture. To understand this is to lead him to appreciate the confusion of children in finding that things they had learnt to despise at home are held in some esteem at school. This should result in a more understanding teacher, probably a more patient one, and, possibly, more effective teaching. Certainly it should help to establish good relations with children and go some way towards winning the acceptance of the values of such a teacher as they are expressed in the curriculum he teaches.

The trap to beware of is that which assumes that the subcultural notions of the teacher have intrinsic superiority over those of the pupils. This, or its converse, is what the sociological approach warns against. And so does Marxism. If a progressive stance is to be sought, it will be found by the application of criticism to the tenets of both subcultures with the promotion of social development as the major objective.

Social structure

The basic units of subcultural living are those items of human behaviour—actions, responses and counter-responses—which are expected and which realise the expectations. The expectations are realised because there is a tendency for the behavioural situation to repeat itself over and over again. Explanations of all kinds are built up for parental, filial, friendship and other social actions and responses. The explanations however, are generally used to justify whatever is done. But the expectation as such arises from the fact that the participants have experienced, repeatedly, just that behaviour and just that response in the recurring situations. This habitual way of living for so much of our time is not at all to be scorned. The unexpected act surprises. A response to it has to be thought about if disorientation and dislocation in life is to be avoided. Far from being a denial of it, the realisation of expectations is a necessary basis for creativity; for without basic habitual action and reaction of the kind outlined neither time nor mental energy would be available for use in selected fields of creative endeavour. Freedom to apply thought and energy in any one direction depends upon economies in time and movement gained from the confidence of habit in the realisation of expectations elsewhere. The expectations then, that situations will tend to recur, and that at longer and shorter, regular and irregular intervals of time, familiar interactions will be induced thereby, arise from the fact that this is generally what happens.

The kind of picture that the culture concept with its subcultural ramifications should conjure up is that of an intricate set of behaviours and interactions, with subsets of such behaviours and interactions being repeated over and over again—albeit with variations—but always recognisable precisely because of the repetition. If we look at this in another way we might see a 'structure' in the complex of repeated behaviours. Indeed, when we use the term 'pattern' or the term 'set' or the term 'relationship' we are using what are more or less synonyms for the same thing: we are imposing a special way of looking at the behaviours of people, at the dynamic, active, and historical phenomena we call culture, insisting upon the expectation of repetition. 'Pattern' and 'structure' are words that call our sense of space and spatial relationships into action in our attempts to conceptualise the actual behaviours of an ongoing society.

In making a graph, when we set out co-ordinate horizontal and vertical axes, organising thereby given data to yield curves of one sort or another we are doing the same sort of thing. In graph-making we use our spatial faculties to help us understand forces at work and trends of movement. But we do not make the mistake of letting the graph become a substitute for, rather than an expression of, the data organised in that way. When we talk about social structure we are using in a similar way our spatial intelligence to give 'shape' to the realities of social phenomena.

What is called social structure then is the positional aspect of culture: what is called culture is the dynamic aspect of social structure. The essential drawback in looking at social phenomena with structure in mind is that false notions of permanence may be encouraged thereby. It is forgotten too often that the behaviours giving rise to set expectations are those of persons, that persons grow up, age and die. They are replaced by others and in this process lies a source of change. Moreover the structure concept is derived from a guess at, or a collection of average behaviours. Since there are always deviations from an average (which need not correspond with any one actual behaviour)—the standard deviation indicating extent and direction of the deviations—another source of change is indicated. Finally, when investigations of the behaviours themselves show us conflicting motivations and/or non-realisable ends, another, more revolutionary, source of change is revealed. In sum, providing that we remember that it is the culture which underlies its structural or positional aspect, we ought to find in structure a useful way of looking at educational processes and institutions.

What Marxism has to add here is that societies, wherein exploitation is part of the culture, part of the ongoing behaviour, generate institutions whose special task it is to maintain the form of exploitation in practice. Those who are in an economically advantageous position create special organisations of persuasion, judgment, punishment and repression in order to perpetuate the structure. To the economic advantage of some groups is added therefore, inevitably, dominance or political power. This power and its officers Marxism calls the state. The goal which is delegated to personnel of the state is to ensure that the repetition of exploitative behaviour goes on without interruption, that is to say, that the social structure will not be fractured. It follows from this that whatever other changes take place in the culture patterns the question of power is crucial to new behaviours obtaining a high enough frequency to characterise society.

Where one form of exploitation is giving way merely to another form accession to political power generally caps the spread of new economic practices and gives them greater momentum. But where the practice of exploitation as such is challenged new economic relationships cannot come into being without their inauguration by a political power already in the hands of the exploited groups. The social structure cannot go through fundamental change of this kind without the substitution for the old form of state, of a new one.

It also follows from what we have said of the state that education and educational institutions tend to play their part in winning support and assent to existing economic and political relationships. The educational structure to a significant degree is part of the state itself.

To inaugurate a non-exploitative society requires the institution of a new kind of state, but one that is unique in the sense of its superfluousness once the new society is structurally sound and guaranteed by what must be a world-wide absence of exploitative practices and states of the old kind. Such inauguration cannot occur without the maturation of certain necessary elements within the social system of class exploitation. Engels in *Socialism: Utopian and Scientific* outlines the process as follows (1969 edn, p.148):

> The abolition of classes in society presupposes a degree of historical evolution at which the existence, not simply of this or that particular ruling class, but of any ruling class at all, and, therefore, the existence of class distinction itself has become an anachronism. It presupposes therefore, the development of production carried out to a degree at which appropriation of the means of production and of the products, and, with this, of political domination, of the monopoly of culture, and of intellectual leadership by a particular class of society, has become not only superfluous but economically, politically, intellectually a hindrance to development.

Socialising agencies

Now socialisation or the transmission of the ongoing meanings of the various subcultures and the culture as a whole takes place in small groups. Society is an idea in the minds of men requiring ability to conceptualise their experience of the entirety of social pressures upon them. These pressures however, are always mediated—exerted by closely associated persons whose demands, hopes, wishes, orders, observed needs, opinions, suggestions, rewards and punishments constitute the force of social pressure. The groups operating as socialising agencies are usefully referred to as primary groups. It is necessary to understand in the case of primary groups to which children belong, that they are called primary groups, not because they are first groups (families) but because they are groups in which social pressures are met at first hand. In the family for example, in the school class, in the peer group, a child finds the same expectations from the same persons in force repeatedly.

In the family parents may be seen as socialising agents. This is not to say that parents make their own expectations or constitute the ultimate source of values determining their duties. They do not. There are many pressures beyond the family which determine the notions firmly held by parents of the responses they should make towards their children's behaviour. The picture of the new-born infant as being utterly helpless and completely at the mercy of what his parents are, is not quite a true one. Parents act largely in accordance with what they believe is expected of them in respect of the upbringing of children. Maps of behavioural expectations on the part of parents from their children, and what they are prepared to do to realise these expectations have been outlined and described by investigators of various cultures and subcultures. A British series of investigations for example, is that made by the team led by John and Elizabeth Newsom, the results of which are outlined in *Patterns of Infant Care in an Urban Community* and *Four Years Old in an Urban Community*, each dealing with its subject in Nottingham. In the former, in chapter 12, the influence of the subculture over parents' expectations is clearly defined as such (1966, p.213):

Many of the class differences which we have found in the way
children are handled can only be interpreted in terms of the more
general differences of the styles of life associated with the
various occupational groups . . . . We tend to live surrounded
by members of our own social class so that pressures are
exerted upon us to conform in our behaviour to the norms of
that class; class differences thus become defined and perpetuated.

The school class is a primary group composed of a number of children usually of the same age with an adult in control—the teacher. Here the main socialising agent is the teacher though the children act upon each other as socialising agents too. The goals of socialisation which the teacher has to aim for are more clearly prescribed than those of the parents, and his role in mediating the pressures of the wider society is more apparent than that of a father or a mother. This is especially so since the force of the school, which may be thought of as a secondary group clearly, stands behind him. The content of socialisation changes of course as children go from one school class to another, but in brief they may be said to comprise: (i) the provision of a mode of childhood currently thought proper for the culture as a whole; (ii) the provision of facilities for certain aspects of child upbringing thought to be necessary; (iii) the inculcation of skills, knowledge and ideas thought of as necessary life-enablements for society later on.

The school class provides opportunities for the formation of peer or friendship groups but it must be stressed that the most powerful socialising influence in the school class is the teacher as one of the managers of the school.

Peer groups are composed of persons who stand in relation to each other, with no institutionalised authority. Any authority which does arise within a peer group springs from the relative intrinsic strengths and weaknesses of its members. The socialisation which goes on in a peer group therefore, is one which prepares children to act and to interact with a progressive reduction of adult guidance and authority. But the consciousness, the values and intentions are derived from meanings employed in family and in school class as well as from the less direct and continuous socialising agencies such as the mass media. Peer groups become, progressively, more and more powerful socialising agencies as children reach adolescence and adulthood.

Where socialisation goes on at first hand the members of the primary group take up the meanings given and act them out each in his or her own specific way. If the group is to continue it must find a way of meeting the pressures external to it. And it must also be able to contain conflicts internal to it. Whatever it does to manage its internal and external continuities it must bring each of the group's members into reciprocity with each other. Indeed it is the complex of reciprocal actions that make the group. Each member is therefore known to every other member by his habitual behaviours. Each behaviour will be—in varying proportions—initiatory and responsive with regard to other behaviours. The bundle of initiatives and responses characteristic of each member of the group is called his role. Where we are dealing with any actual group—e.g. the Jones family as distinct from family in general—role and identity are the same. Whether in co-operation, in competition or in antagonism—or in combinations of all three—the role, or identity, of each group member will be the outcome, overwhelmingly, of his or her personal history in primary groups.

Institutions and roles

It is now necessary to look at roles in another way, and we have prepared for this, partly, by our definition of structure as the positional aspect of culture. We said that it was repeated repetition of an action or of an interaction that gave it pattern—that these repetitions were to be found not only in one group but in other groups also. For example, children's going to school from Monday to Friday is practised by those of every family. If the count of the number of persons repeatedly acting in the same way (of children going to school, of workers joining unions, of couples getting married) is called a frequency, we shall see that there is a point at which that frequency is so high as to become characteristic of the culture.

Where the practice has become characteristic, that is to say has a high frequency, we can declare that it has become an institution— has become institutionalised.

If the question is put, 'organisation or activity?' the answer is 'Both!' A religion to exist must have believers believing and must organise the belief and the practice. Similarly, a trade union to exist as an organisation must have practitioners of trade unionism in factories and workshops for it to be an institution. We return to the formula: there is a positional (organisational) aspect for every behavioural (activity) pattern, and a behavioural (activity) aspect for every organisation.

Thus families, schools, clubs, shops, trade unions, factories, farms, town councils, political parties, are all institutions which may be thought of in terms of what the persons involved in them are doing. More generally they may be thought of as organisations wherein and whereby typical forms of action and interaction are promoted. The 'wherein' part looks at action and interaction internal to the institution, the 'whereby' part looks at action undertaken in relation to other institutions and the natural environment. What happens within an institution may support or hinder its activities externally: what happens externally may support or hinder activities within an institution.

In its particular ways then, each and every institution interlocks, meshes, with every other institution. This does not mean that all institutions have equal weight. The inequality becomes plain when we study the reciprocal influences of factories and families or of schools and families. Family life is conducted in such a way as to make work possible and in such a way as to make school life possible. Strains will arise, but for stability in the social structure to endure, the strains imposed by institutions on each other must be such as to be bearable. Marxists add to this formula the observations that the interactions pertaining to economic institutions in class societies involve exploitation, that these interactions beget, perpetually, antagonistic interests between the opposing classes, that institutions arise to sustain the conflicting interests and that from an ultimately final struggle between the warring classes arises a new overall structure with an impulse to the creation of appropriate, new institutions.

It is now possible to redeem the promise to look at role in another way. We have thought of role as encompassing what is relevant to any one group-member's meanings for the rest and for himself. But if practices are repeated and have a high frequency, if kinds of groups and the activities they organise are institutionalised, the same must be said of roles. In other words, we can, in a way, separate what is institutional about a role from the way in which a particular person performs it. Thus, we could have no notion of a teacher's role, or a father's role, or an employer's role, without the many teachers, fathers, employers behaving as they do in society. But we would expect to find on the part of any one teacher, father, employer, peculiarities not to be included in the notion held of the institutionalised role.

This is the source of the concept of norm. The idea commonly held of how a teacher should behave is derived from the mode—a kind of average—of how teachers actually do behave. The norm is the criterion by which successful performance of the institutionalised role is judged. There are many kinds of pressures at work to prevent teachers, headmasters, parents, children from departing too radically from the norms in force. There are the external pressures in the case of teachers, exerted by children, other teachers, parents, the press, films, education reports, researches, examinations, inspectors, and so on. But another powerful pressure comes from the teacher himself who has internalised the norm in such a way as to make it his own ideal.

Institutionalised roles may be few or many. There is only one Secretary of State for Education and Science, but the institutionalised expectations of the Secretary, as well as the institutionalised expectations upon him, limit and define what he will do. The headmaster, as a type is more numerous. But the same is true of that role as of the role with greater power. Just as the one realises and makes effective political expectations connected with education and the educational system, so the latter realises and makes effective expectations connected with the school.

Roles and statuses

We ought now to see what the idea of social structure does for institutionalised or typed roles. We stressed earlier that structure is the positional aspect of culture, culture the behavioural aspect of structure. We deliberately held to the dynamics of society, to its cultural aspect when we involved ourselves with roles and norms. If we turn from this to try to discover where roles fit into structure we shall find that we are looking for positions in that structure. The position a role finds in a structure is a status. More exactly, status is the positional aspect of role, role is the behavioural aspect of status.

There are roles and statuses of many kinds. Some are associated with age so that special behaviours are seen to be appropriate to various stages of childhood, to middle age, to old age. For educationists and for parents a special problem arises here. Some cultures do not know adolescence as a special role or status: initiation into adulthood is short and sharp. And some of our own subcultures only admit a very short adolescence. More and more however, our culture tends to delay adult roles. The raising of the school leaving age to sixteen and the rapid increase in numbers staying on till eighteen are indicative of this. We are beginning to think along lines which may result in a general acceptance of study as a form of work. This is facilitated by the grant system, by the lowering of the age of majority, and by the ways in which students assert themselves. There are still those however who impose financial dependence upon young people on the one hand whilst expecting mature behaviour on the other.

Then there are roles and statuses associated with sex. These are perhaps more clearly defined in simpler societies. But they unmistakably exist in our own. Masculinity and femininity are not simply attributes of sex, they are also patterns of activity normally expected of each other by the men and women of a given culture. When we are engaged in bringing up or in educating boys and girls we find ourselves pressed into assuming or adapting to the appropriate norms. This is expressed in curriculum provision as much as it is expressed in behaviours of a more diffuse kind.

Men and women, boys and girls belong to more than one group. Since each person has a role in a group it therefore follows that he has multiple roles and statuses. Naturally, not every role is fully active at the same time. When it is not active it is said to be latent. From the teacher's point of view it is regularly necessary to persuade children that a certain active role should be made latent—as when playtime is over—and it is occasionally thought useful to delay the assumption of a valued active role as a kind of negative sanction or punishment. In special cases when we know that a child is just overcoming difficulties in winning acceptance from the group, an observant teacher might be patient in organising the switching of roles that must occur. But we should also realise that the activities within the classroom—or rather the activities organised there—do not have to exclude altogether the following of roles largely elaborated in the peer group. Group work and team work by children may be so arranged as to make good use of spontaneous informal friendships.

But the most important use of the idea of latent and active role has a negative and a positive direction. The idea should help a teacher take guard against the depreciation of roles which are active for a child at home, and it should remind the teacher that there is a vast source of meanings which is immediately available to a child. The experience of children outside school should be an inspiration for work in the classroom and should be enlightened by what goes on there. Formally stated, latent roles should be activated by the teacher to serve the requirements of a learning situation.

Another notion associated with role and status draws attention to the fact that any one role, any one status can only be fully understood if it is seen within a role-set, within an array of statuses. Mr Jones is the husband of Mrs Jones; he is also the father of his daughter of seventeen and of his son of fifteen. To define his family situation with some kind of precision we should call him a husband-father (a)—father (b) just as Mrs Jones should be called a wife-mother (a)—mother (b). A teacher's role-set and array of statuses involves not only interaction between a child and him, but inter-action also between the group and the teacher, between parents and teacher, colleagues and teacher, headmaster and teacher, local authority and teacher, teachers' association and teacher. The set of roles on the school premises is especially worthy of note for it is here that a teacher can make a vital contribution to the evolution of teaching norms.

The notion of role-set and array of statuses makes it possible for the teacher to map his own position in the school and in the pro-fession. Using the same concept he is helped to appreciate better the situation affecting the children with whom he interacts and that of his professional associates.

We select two other role concepts important to an understanding of the socialisation process and we take them together because they stand in opposition to each other. These are ascribed role and status and achieved role and status. Roles and statuses in respect of age and sex are largely ascribed. The role and status of schoolboy is ascribed, so is the house-keeping role as understood by the wife-mother. In a caste society where the children follow strictly in the footsteps of their parents, occupation is somewhat strictly ascribed. But although the role of schoolboy is ascribed that of grammar-schoolboy is achieved. We live in a society where, because occu-pational role and status is increasingly achieved rather than ascribed and because the achievement is facilitated by performance at school, achievement occupies a central position in the scale of values in force in the educational world.

This kind of achievement is not of the kind which can be as characteristic of ascribed role as it can be of achieved role. An ascribed role can be done well or it can be done badly; that is to say, a high standard of achievement can be reached in the performance of an ascribed role just as a poor standard can characterise an achieved role. A Marxist view is that there exists a major tension, a continuous conflict between two tendencies generated in our schools: one insists that teachers should aim in all schools for high achievement on the part of all our children, in knowledge, in skill, in aesthetic awareness, in understanding and in life generally; another insists that teachers should aim in all schools to grade children, to stimulate competition, to have children *achieve against each other* for purposes of ultimate occupational allocation.

To be aware that this latter pressure is an inevitable result of a society whose occupational roles and statuses are hierarchically arranged can have important consequences. First, such awareness can induce a degree of caution with regard to an easy acceptance by the teacher of his role as a selector. Second, it may bring him to look critically at the entirety of his society and to search out the means whereby these pressures—at odds with education in its former sense—might be reduced, or even ended.

Chapter 3

Industrial societies and education

Characteristics of industrial societies

When we discussed the culture concept we said that one advantage to be derived from it ought to be that of being able to look at our own culture, and the implication was that we might be able to do so with a degree of detachment. Now the society in which we live has been called 'industrial society'. But when we use this term we should be quite clear that no society is adequately described by it. It is not even adequately described when it is called a 'capitalist society' or a 'socialist society'. But at least when the term capitalism or socialism is used we are not shirking the issue of pointing at the locus of economic and political power in that society. As an example of the kind of limitation which still remains there is the question of the form that power may take.

But if the description of an overall pattern of culture is incomplete when the institutions of power are left out, is there any purpose in discussing industrial society? There is, providing we bear in mind that when we are talking about an industrial society we are considering its technology and the direct influence of that technology on other institutions.

The main characteristics of industrial society may be said to be as follows:

(1) institutions where work activities are organised tend to grow in size. There are establishments employing tens of thousands of workers;

(2) the number of work organisation units tends to diminish—production is concentrated;

(3) in any economy the labour force is distributed in three major

sectors: primary production (agriculture, mining, forestry, fishing), secondary production (manufacture), and finally, services and professions. In an industrial economy numbers employed in primary production tend to shrink, services and professions tend to expand at the expense mainly of the primary sector;

(4) the state as an institution of government tends to extend its area of legitimate action and assumes increasing responsibility especially for the direction of the economy;

(5) the division of labour in production, in the provision of services and in the professions is intensified—that is, specialisation becomes more and more dominant;

(6) new techniques in every social sphere, but especially in production, give rise to new forms of employment and to new roles in society;

(7) the changes in techniques based upon the application of scientific knowledge to problems of production give rise to structural change in the economy and in society;

(8) the rate of such change accelerates and creates special problems in the preparation of new recruits to roles and statuses in the economy;

(9) increase of output, rise in productivity, becomes an aim deliberately motivating the economy whose health or richness is judged by the rate of increase of production. The years 1960–5 witnessed the following scale of growth in three countries: 17 per cent in the United Kingdom, 32 per cent in the USA and 51 per cent in the USSR.

(10) specialisation in production tends to take on world proportions; the world division of labour intensifies;

(11) this is expressed in the existence of a world market, in trading agreements between governments, between governments and firms, and between firms and firms;

(12) towns and cities grow, conurbations develop and even account for the habitation of a preponderance of the population;

(13) enormous consumptions of fossil energy (coal, oil, gas) and of other materials together with equally massive outputs of waste create severe ecological problems;

(14) The administration of industry, of the economy, of urban complexes and of governmental institutions entails the emergence of large and complex bureaucracies whose work can only be carried out on the basis of precisely defined terms of reference;

(15) education for more and more members of the society to standards typical of what is called higher education becomes vital for the maintenance of the economy;

(16) in line with the general development of bureaucracies, the unification and extension of education into educational systems create complex educational bureaucracies;

(17) communications of every kind tend to become more efficient;

(18) mass media as a special case of efficient communication become a significant factor in the socialisation process.

These are the major characteristics of industrial society but only some of them will be selected for special elaboration. The increase in the size of the firm, for example, is of special importance because this has proceeded side by side with a diminishing number of people whose work could be done at home. Effectively, industrialisation has separated the place of work from the home so that the family's productive activities are not what they were. Work is, in the main, carried on in non-kinship units. Two other factors which have affected family interaction are (i) increased concentration of production and (ii) structural changes in industry consequent upon changing techniques. These taken together have led to considerable geographical mobility of labour.

The connection between this and the small family whose household excludes the parents of the spouses as well as their brothers and sisters is simply that this kind of family finds it easier to move around. Again increasing specialisation and the proliferation of new techniques make it easier for sons to decline to follow in their fathers' footsteps. Nucleation occurs during the dispersal stage of the family. The family then tends to become nuclear, to consist of husband-father, wife-mother and children.

Another of the characteristics we should look at more closely is the distribution of the labour force. Table 1 shows the trend in industrial Britain for the tertiary sector of the economy to grow at the expense of the primary sector.

But this table is not the whole story. If we examine the structural changes in manpower in what are called the metal industries, covering metal manufacture, engineering and electrical goods, shipbuilding and marine engineering, vehicles and metal goods we shall be considering a sector of the economy with over four million employees in 1963 (4,339,000), nearly 20 per cent of all employed personnel (19·3 per cent).

Now the report entitled *Manpower Studies* (Ministry of Labour, 1965) *No. 2* has to say that due to technological change, increases in employment that might have been derived from expansion in demand have been largely offset so that the total rise in employment from 1958 to 1963 was only 4·4 per cent. The technological change referred to included automation and the use of the computer.

White collar or clerical workers in the industry increased as a share of the labour force, skilled operatives diminished as a proportion of the labour force. At the same time, 'Qualified scientists, professional engineers and other technologists increased their numbers by 28%' (ibid. p.14) and the report goes on to comment that in all other industries the number of scientists and technologists increased much faster than the total labour force.

TABLE 1   *Employees in employment**
United Kingdom (000,000)

Industry	(a)	(b)	(c)	(d)
	1953	1959	1969	% change (a)—(c)
Mining and quarrying	8·8	8·3	6·9	—6·9
Agriculture, fishing, and forestry	7·5	6·5	5·6	—25·2
Construction	13·3	12·7	13·7	+ 3·0
Food, drink, tobacco	8·3	8·1	8·3	No change
Metal, ship repair, and engineering	31·0	33·0	35·0	+12·6
Gas, electric, water	3·8	3·8	4·0	+ 5·3
Vehicles	8·4	8·7	8·7	+ 3·6
Textiles	10·3	8·9	8·3	—19·5
Clothing	6·6	5·7	5·7	—16·7
Other manufacture	19·6	20·4	21·4	+ 9·2
Distribution	22·7	27·5	29·6	+39·7
Public administration	13·5	12·7	13·7	+ 1·5
Professional and scientific services	15·5	18·6	22·6	+45·7

*Source: Ministry of Labour, *Manpower studies No.1*, HMSO, 1964 (percentages added)

Now technologists are people who have very high qualifications—possibly of degree standard. But there are people employed with intermediate qualifications who are called technicians. The report points out that between 1958 and 1963 their number rose by 31 per cent—even faster than the number of technologists. It continues: 'In most industries the increase was in the region of 30% or more'. (ibid.).

The essential lesson to be learnt from this is that our industrial society's economy is demanding a progressively higher proportion of highly qualified personnel in the labour force.

Industrial societies and education

What does this mean for education? Well one thing it has meant is the rejection of the notion that there is only a limited pool of ability available to the society. Industrial society in its most recent developments constitutes a culture which cannot accept, in the long run, the belief that only a tiny proportion of its children and young people can grasp the meanings which inhere in higher education. The 1950s was the first decade where this rejection was explicitly pronounced. *Early Leaving* (DES, 1954) and the Crowther Report (DES, 1959) were the first reports to suggest unlimited resources of mental ability. Plowden quotes Crowther with approval (DES, 1967, vol.1, pp.30–1):

It may well be that there is a pool of ability that imposes an upper limit on what can be done by education at any given time. But if so, it is sufficiently clear that the limit has not been reached and will not even be approached without much more in the way of inducement and opportunity.

The Robbins Report (DES, 1963b, Appendix I, p.79) declares that it is not 'possible to tell what proportion of the population are so constituted at birth, that growing up under the most favourable circumstances they could reach a level of attainment suitable for entry to higher education'.

Indeed it is a feature of the history of education over the last twenty years that the dire need of the economy for more and more highly qualified personnel has shifted attention away from the problem of what limitations there may be on the pool of ability towards the waste of ability and the crippling of ability our educational institutions are prone to. This change of focus is not seen in all quarters as an issue of social evolution which permits human fulfilment on a higher level of intellectual and aesthetic awareness than before. It is rather taken to mean that opportunities are there and seen to be there for those knocking on the door with one hand and holding qualifications with the other. As a consequence parents are willing to keep their children at school beyond the statutory leaving age and young people increasingly see the advantages of staying on at school.

The demand for educational expansion therefore has two great elemental sources in industrial societies: the needs of the economy, the aspirations of the young and their parents.

This is a great boon to those educationists and others who strive for a widening of educational facilities on quite other grounds. Some believe that education is good for the person who has it, and thereby good for society. Others believe that a real democracy can only come into being when the majority are educated and articulate because only then can they participate in decision-making. What is certainly true however, is that there has been an 'education explosion' over the past twenty years and that these forces are the major determinants of this social fact: the need for highly qualified workers, the readiness of young people and adults to become qualified, the willingness of educationalists to expand the educational institutions.

Moreover, education must begin to be pursued for quite other reasons than as a means to the end of securing privileged occupational status. This is because: (i) the very increase in output of highly qualified persons will inevitably, in a capitalist economy, reduce their market value; (ii) this fact impels the educated to seek to be valued on account of their social use; (iii) the widespread norm of social intercourse requiring high levels of literacy must eventually move people to want higher educational levels; (iv) industrial societies of a socialist sort will gradually create new normative systems corresponding to conditions where the essentials of life are no longer in scarce supply.

An examination of the technical aspects of industrial society yields sufficient explanation for the expansion of educational institutions. And the faster the rate of technological change the greater that expansion must be. But we have to look at other characteristics of industrial society if we are to understand ourselves and the groups and individuals who compose it. We have to study the kinds of consciousness and value orientations that seem to be thrown up by industrial societies. Since we are concerned with education, what is used in this discussion is highly selective, the selection of ideas being directed towards enlightening an overall view of educational practice and endeavour.

Organic solidarity and education

One outstanding sociologist whose understanding of modern society has illuminated educational thought is Emile Durkheim. His view was that sparsity of population in earlier or less developed societies was such as to compel every man to be more or less competent to perform a wide range of tasks and every woman similarly. That is to say, there was a very simple division of labour. And this ensured that social institutions in such societies would be more or less like each other. An early or simple or pre-literate society therefore would be segmental in pattern, each institution organised more or less like the next and performing more or less the same range of activities.

From this sameness of the basic units of society, each carrying out almost a full range of essential functions of life there has been built up a view of society in which there were: (i) no question of occupational choice; (ii) little or no diversity of status in adulthood; (iii) no need to prepare for a choice; (iv) no aspiration to upward mobility; (v) only one mode of adulthood personified in the father (or maternal uncle) for a boy, in the mother for a girl. Relationships within these institutions were therefore fixed on a firm basis of authority wielded by adult kin and of reciprocal loyalty from the young. Relationships between institutions were fixed on a basis of little differentiation of task where collective effort was necessary or believed to be so. The mode of solidarity in such a society was, therefore, according to Durkheim, mechanical solidarity.

The pressures of increase of population and of increase of density of population were, according to Durkheim, the main sources of differentiation of task or of a social division of labour. On this view technological development would be an outcome of population increase. Whatever the connection may be between technology and population the two certainly tend to coincide and there is no doubt about specialisation of social purposes. Workplaces are separated from living places, schools replace homes as bases for formal education, infant welfare becomes a professional study, nurses take over the task of tending the sick from mothers, wives and daughters, old people are looked after in homes and so on.

What is characteristic then of a society with a high density of population is that there is a great variety of social institutions. The pattern yielded is not segmental but organic, with each type of institution fulfilling a function in relation to the functions of others.

From the description of organic society there has been built up a view of life which includes meanings to the effect that: (i) occupation is largely a matter of choice; (ii) a diversity of statuses in adulthood arises on the basis of specialisation; (iii) a minimum level of generalised skills relevant to work has to be acquired during childhood; (iv) aspiration towards valued statuses flourishes; (v) immediate adult relatives cease to be the only models of adult roles. The variation in types of institutions also means that relationships within any one institution are affected by those within others and within any institution account has to be taken of roles elsewhere.

As for relationships between institutions, since their functions have to relate to each other, mechanisms for the regulation of these relationships have to arise. The mode of solidarity in an organic society is seen to be organic solidarity.

For Durkheim, 'Since the division of labour becomes the chief source of social solidarity, it becomes, at the same time the foundation of the moral order' (1947 edn, p.400). What society of an industrial type compels therefore, is that on the one hand we become expert in a given mode of activity, on the other, that we accept the consensus of values currently established by the society as a whole. 'We must . . . contract our horizon, choose a task, immerse in it, completely.' and 'We ought so to work as to realise in ourselves the collective type as it exists' with its 'common sentiments, ideas without which one is not a man' (ibid., p.401).

It has been said that the usefulness for education of the segmental-mechanical solidarity/organic-organic solidarity axis is that it is directly applicable to schools. An article by Basil Bernstein in *New Society* of 14 September 1967 details the way in which segmental schools with mechanical solidarity are giving way to schools as organic societies motivated by organic solidarity.

It would appear however that the notions which Bernstein infers from Durkheim's theories were not what were intended. Durkheim had a distinctly authoritarian standpoint with regard to education. He unfolded his fundamental notions in relation to the roles of both teacher and child in lectures some of which are now brought together in a volume entitled *Education and Sociology* (1956 edn). Here education is defined as 'the influence exercised by adult generations on those not ready for social life'. Its purpose is 'to arouse and develop in the child . . . physical, intellectual and moral states which are demanded of him by both the political society as a whole and the special milieu for which he is specifically destined.' Children are not active beings assimilating and influencing their culture: each new generation, 'is a tabula rasa, very nearly, on which [society] must build anew' (p.72). The teacher is like a 'hypnotiser [who] must speak in a commanding tone, with authority, indicating that refusal to obey is not even conceivable' (p.85). 'Education must be essentially a matter of authority' (p.87).

The teacher, explains Durkheim, 'Above all . . . must feel in himself the authority the feeling for which he is trying to transmit'. 'He is the agent of a great moral person: society' (pp.88–9). That society, that moral person is manifest in the state whose duty it is to tell the teacher what must be done (pp.79–80).

If education has a collective function . . . (it is impossible for society not to be interested). . . . It is then up to the state to remind the teacher constantly of the ideas sentiments, that must be impressed upon the child.

It will be seen that there is nothing here to coincide with the child-centredness characterising Bernstein's orientation.

Durkheim expected increasing division in the organisation of education. In terms of modern Britain his logic leads to an expectation of an extension of streaming in the junior school and a greater differentiation of secondary schools. But the trend has been in the opposite direction, towards the 'common school' in both primary and secondary stages. Moreover as Benn and Simon indicate in *Half-Way There* (1970) the trend is world wide. But Durkheim holds that there is 'no society in which different pedagogical systems do not co-exist'—because there is no society in which there is no division of labour. What differs between pre-industrial and industrial societies is the condition of entry. In the past children entered a particular system according to criteria established by birth. In industrial society—in this case France—'Even if education of our children should not depend upon the chance of birth . . . education would not become more uniform. Though the career of each child would no longer be determined by heredity, occupational specialisation would not fail to result in a great pedagogical diversity.' For Britain such a perspective would have been realised in an extension of the principles underlying the tripartite system and prepared for by streamed primary schools.

In general, plausible though Durkheim's ideas may be, apart from the coincidence of population growth with industrial development they lack historical verification or usefulness as an interpretive tool. The antagonisms between developed and under-developed societies, between the industrial societies themselves, and within each industrial society are not explained by the antithesis of mechanical and organic solidarity. They fail to be explained because Durkheim furnishes no treatment of the way in which the history of the social division of labour begets variations in the degree of power associated with each of the divisions whether in his segmental, poly-segmental, or organic societies. The deficiency is emphasised by the absence of consideration concerning the evolution of a specific division whose particular work is the exercise of power.

By contrast, Engels in the *Origin of the Family, Private Property and the State* (1972 edn, ch. ix) makes the 'first great social division of labour' between pastoralists and food-gatherers, the 'second great division of labour' between handicrafts and agriculturists. The third division of labour however 'creates a class which no longer concerns itself with production, but only with the exchange of products—the merchants.' Following Marx, Engels shows that it is the product surplus to immediate needs, its ownership, its accumulation and its disposal which is the determinant of new social relationships and further social divisions of labour. Engels goes on to show that the state, a public force, arises to keep in check the consequent antagonisms between the classes which have come into existence. However, as the state 'also arose in the thick of the fight between the classes, it is normally the state of the most powerful, economically dominant class . . . and so acquires new means of holding down and exploiting the oppressed class' (ibid., p.231).

Universalism, specificity and achievement

Another view of industrial society, which corresponds in many respects with the standpoints of Durkheim, helps us to understand the value orientations generated by its role system. Parsons says of the industrial occupational structure that (1951, pp.177–8):

Its primary characteristic is a system of universalistic-specific-affectively neutral achievement roles. There must not only be particular roles of this type but they must fit together into complex systems both within the same organisation and within the ecological complexes linking individuals and organisations together. . . . It is out of the question for such a role system to be directly homologous with a kinship structure so that it should be essentially a network of interlocking kinship units as many other social structures like the feudal tend to be.

Roles which are universalistic should be seen to involve their actors in meanings and attitudes which stand in direct contrast with roles which are particularistic, Universalistic behaviour is that which sets aside immediate, personal, familial or friendship group needs to satisfy those of the firm, of the nation, of society, whereas particularistic behaviour does the opposite.

Thus to the particularistically oriented miner, the basic purpose of his going to work is wages, and what is the use of a good wage if he cannot, when he feels like it, take Monday off. Increased productivity as a national goal does not have the same value for him as it has for an economist in the employ of the National Coal Board. The latter, universalistically oriented, will be disposed to berate absenteeism, effectively reflecting other values.

Linked with universalistic roles are achievement roles. We have noted that roles (and therefore statuses) may be ascribed or achieved. In an industrial society, superior statuses, carrying with them more privileges and/or greater esteem than others, demand from their would-be occupants the kind of self-discipline and effort over shorter or longer periods which lead to qualifications. Only possessors of symbols of achievement—certificates, diplomas, degrees, etc.—are judged eligible for consideration even for training as practitioners of a variety of occupational roles. The Crowther Report remarks (DES, 1959, p.48).

Not so very long ago, there were very few qualifications below those of the professions, save those that could be secured by merely serving in a given status for a stated length of time, as in many apprenticeships. Now there are scores of thousands of boys, and a smaller but steadily growing number of girls, in every type of school, who have a specific qualification of one kind or another in view. Two separate trends have combined to produce the same result. In the first place there has been a rapid rise in the number of jobs that cannot be performed without some special knowledge or experience. In addition to this, however, there is a growing tendency for many occupations which do not absolutely require a specific expertise for their performance, nevertheless to demand an attested standard of general education for entrance.

Apart from certificates, once having entered the work force, the employee is expected to seek promotion, to climb—or, at least, to want to. It is clear that this kind of social mobility cannot take place if the impulse to do so is not accompanied by universalistic orientations. Hence it is clear that universalistic achievement orientations encourage a complex of attitudes which result in certain choices from the range of possible actions inherent in any given situation. Industrial society normalises ambition. Indeed, as Professor Ralph Turner points out, those who see no point in getting on are likely to be regarded as deviants.

Specificity is directly connected with (i) the division of labour, (ii) the compartmentalisation of knowledge which accompanies specialisation (and diversity) of research, (iii) the need for precision in the space-time arrangements and in the quantity-quality performances made necessary by a highly complex society. Imperfect mastery of a great variety of skills, vague formulae and beliefs concerning forces of nature, absence of legal definition concerning interpersonal and social relationships, blurring of occupational and other roles and statuses by their containment in kinship institutions, all work reasonably well in pre-industrial societies. But in face of the issues set forth by industrial society, diffuseness gives way to specificity.

The final term of Parsons's formula is affective neutrality. Quite simply this means that in matters of employment, in business generally, and in dealings with administrative bureaucracies, preferment may be justified only by reference to fitness according to qualification and ability—not as deemed by feelings or likings. Personality, likeableness or disagreeableness, do, of course, enter into the making of decisions as to who will gain a post for which several applicants have been interviewed. But industrial society does determine eligibility for more and more jobs by reference to criteria which exclude affective states of mind. Examinations have come into being partly in order to remove the chance of affective predisposition when the qualification symbols are awarded. A norm of affective neutrality is expected to govern selection from eligible candidates for positions, and is one measure used to assess the justness of attitude when the choice is made.

The relevance of the formula for education is clear. Universalism is realised in the existence of the schools. In pre-industrial societies the progress from childhood to the practice of adult occupational roles was very largely a particularistic progress, a learning from parents. The proliferation of occupational roles attendant on industrialisation necessitated teaching the basic universalistic skills involved in most of these, literacy and numeracy. Hence the unacceptability of the transfer to industrial society of the practice of children learning overwhelmingly from their parents.

But universalism has expressions other than those pointed to by Parsons. The direct exploitation of children by factory owners proved to be unacceptable to wage labouring parents as well as to some philanthropists whose universalism in this connection began to consider children, not merely as progeny of a substratum of society, but as children. Over and above ran the universalistic pressures of capitalism, the first form of industrial society, for certain requirements to be met. Industry and commerce required educational institutions which would shape a labour force whose education at various levels could be relied upon. The legal-economic order demanded that there be taught the ethic governing 'freedom of contract' between employer and worker, landlord and tenant, pawnbroker and borrower. The politico-civil order expected that social equality be understood in the existence of formally equal rights universally held. The occupational hierarchy sought a system of education in which 'equality of opportunity' obscured the rejection of the majority. These were the social bases of a universalistic educational arrangement according to which it was expected that every child would go to school. Shipman points out (1971, p.150),

> The outline of a school system was visible at the start of the Victorian era...[and]...Although progress was slow, there was by 1945 a state school system that provided a number of different opportunities and experiences for the entire child population.

In the school system universalism may be seen to be progressively operative in curricula, in organisation, in modes of administration, in rules of procedure and in norms of teaching. Meanwhile examinations constitute goals for achievement and criteria of selection for the different streams and the different secondary schools, the various colleges and universities that make up educational systems in capitalist industrial societies.

Nowadays schools are expected to be more permissive than they once were. Teachers are expected to display affection for the pupils and to establish warm relationships with them. But the affective neutrality so vital to being fair in any system of selection is not impaired by the willingness of those who administer rewards to be kind to both achievers and non-achievers.

It will be seen therefore that the value orientations prized by industrial society: universalism, achievement, specificity, affective neutrality, are fostered by an educational system whose growth is so characteristic of that society. It will also be seen that capitalism gives a special slant to these norms. Shipman puts the matter as follows (pp.54–5):

> Competence and personal achievement have become increasingly the product of adequate schooling. Punctuality, quiet, orderly work in large groups, response to orders, bells and time-tables, respect for authority, even tolerance of monotony, boredom, punishment, lack of reward and regular attendance at place of work are habits to be learned in school.

Class struggle and education

It has been remarked that discussions on trends in industrial societies tend to forget conflicting interests and the force or power available to contending groups. When these elements are added to the complex movement from the particularism of feudalism to the universalism of capitalist industrial society the dramatic nature of the change is instantly appreciated. Marx and Engels wrote in the *Manifesto of the Communist Party* (1969 edn, p.51):

> The bourgeoisie, wherever it has got the upper hand, has put an end to all feudal, patriarchal, idyllic relations. It has pitilessly torn asunder the motley feudal ties that bound man to his 'natural superiors' and has left no other nexus between man and man . . . than callous 'cash payment'. . . . It has resolved personal worth into exchange value, and in place of the numberless indefeasible chartered freedoms, has set up that unconscionable freedom—free trade. In one word, for exploitation veiled by religious and poetic illusions, it has substituted naked, shameless, direct, brutal exploitation.

The more inclusive method of analysis is better because it makes it easier to understand real historical events whether past or current. It also enables a more accurate development of strategies for future social change. In this connection it is possible to show that universalistic orientations will be stronger in a socialist society than they are in capitalist society. Thus Marx (1926 edn, vol. II, p.138):

Book-keeping as the control and ideal synthesis of the (productive) process becomes the more necessary the more the process assumes a social scale and loses its purely individual character. It is therefore more necessary in capitalist production than in the scattered production of handicraft and peasant economy, more necessary in collective production than in capitalist production.

Marx has made a very special contribution to the way in which nearly everyone now thinks about society. He and Friedrich Engels formulated the theory that techniques of production constitute the foundation of any social structure and that to suit these techniques an appropriate pattern of economic relationships becomes necessary. These relationships make up the basis of society. In turn, these give rise to a political apparatus, a legal structure and an ideology to protect and to justify the economic arrangements which had been called into existence by the technology and mode of production.

In the famous passage in the Preface to the *Introduction to a Critique of Political Economy* Marx wrote his formula (1918 edn, p.12):

In the social production which men carry on, they enter into definite relations that are indispensable and independent of their will; these relations of production correspond to a definite stage of development of their material power of produc- tion. The sum total of these relations of production constitute the economic structure of society—the real foundation, on which rise legal and political superstructures and to which correspond definite forms of consciousness.

So far so good. We can easily see how economic developments have resulted in demand for a more highly educated population and we can understand economic forces as determinants of educational institutions and how all this conditions what we think about. But Marx also held that the major thrust for social change comes from the same source (ibid.):

At a certain stage of their development, the material forces of
production come into conflict with the existing relations of
production, or . . . with the property relations within which
they had been at work before. From forms of development of
the forces of production these relations turn into their fetters.
Then comes the period of social revolution. With the change of
the economic foundation the entire immense superstructure is
more or less transformed.

But Marx never regarded this as an automatic process. The
preface just quoted was written in 1859. Eleven years earlier in the
Manifesto of the Communist Party Marx and Engels expressed the
view that social revolution was the culmination of class struggle. The
victory of the bourgeoisie over the feudal aristocracy is sketched and
the nature of capitalism is outlined. But within capitalism there rages
another class war: that between the capitalist class and the working
class. This is of central importance for the sociology of education
because the history of education over the last 150 years as well as its
current problems may be seen as one front in that same class
struggle. Is the provision of educational facilities unaffected by the
possession or absence of wealth? Have the controversies over public
schools and comprehensives nothing to do with easily defined class
interests? Are curricula always free from kinds of assumption
supporting capitalism as a system? Are there in force constraints
upon teachers to be upholders of values which promote the interests
of the ruling class? Above all, what truth is there in the assertion that
educational institutions are mainly concerned—not with developing
abilities, awareness, and knowledge in human beings—but with
selecting, at successive stages, a decreasing number of pupils or
students for statuses increasingly higher in the hierarchy of
occupations characteristic of capitalism?

All these questions may be answered so that education is understood to be an area of antagonism between the bourgeoisie and the
proletariat. For success in its struggle what matters most in working-
class thought is the spread and level of its own self-awareness as a
class, of its class consciousness. This applies to short-term interests
and to limited areas of action such as education. It is of paramount
importance for the building of a new society.

The times have changed the nature of the accusation that the
bourgeoisie could level at the communists when the *Manifesto* was
published in 1847. They have not changed its retort (1969 edn, p.66):

But you will say we destroy the most hallowed of relations when we replace home education by social.

And your education! Is not that also social, and determined by the social conditions under which you educate, by the intervention, direct or indirect, of society by means of schools etc? The communists have not invented the intervention of society in education; they do but seek to alter the character of that intervention, and to rescue education from the influence of the ruling class.

Chapter 4

Social mobility or social revolution?

Achievement and social class

Our discussion on the value system promoted in capitalist society gave considerable weight to achievement orientation and there can be no doubt about importance of achievement in schools, in the educational system generally speaking and in the occupations followed later on. Neither is the fostering of ambition restricted only to school performance and preparation for the workaday world. Business, politics and the various 'services', indeed every sphere of social life, seem to place achievement motivation very high in the order of values by which personality and behaviour are judged.

We must be clear about the kind of ambition we are talking about. To grow flowers is an achievement of a kind. To grow more, even more beautiful flowers is a greater achievement of the same kind. But to be recognised as a competent grower of beautiful flowers is another kind of achievement. Yet, it is neither creation nor recognition which is in mind when orientation to achievement is remarked upon as a major characteristic of value-orientation in an industrial society particularly of the capitalist variety.

The achievement here is connected with the positions that in their totality make up the social structure—positions, it should be remembered, which continuously take their shape from the habitual practice, the culture patterns of the institutions that make up society. Since every culture outlives any one of its members, and since every member occupies a position, three things follow: (i) the positions appear to have a certain permanence, (ii) the positions appear to be separable from their incumbents, (iii) the positions are continually vacated and filled again.

But it is seldom in any society a matter of taking out one plug and fitting another. So complex are the expectations from any role-performance that the incumbent of the position associated with it must undergo the special socialisation procedures that prepare for it. Moreover, it must be supposed, from the continuation of the culture, that expectations of any institutionalised role are more or less continuously met and that the role itself has always an 'actor'. This indicates that 'recruits' are always being prepared to take up the positions that make up society.

Given a society with some development in the division of labour, one important form of movement is entry to, or change in, occupation. Now theoretically at least, a society may be envisaged where the division of labour does not involve the attachment of degrees of worth to each occupation. In such a society an occupation could not become a major determinant of the worth of its incumbent: the factors to be considered in problems of occupational allocation could be only the current social requirements, the abilities of the person not positioned, and his own partialities.

What we have to consider, however, is that in pre-industrial societies, and in industrial societies whether capitalist or socialist (as yet) occupations are arranged in an order of worth. We must take into account also that the social division of labour, as distinct from its technical division, extends the term 'occupation' to include the various social classes: lords and knights as well as peasants and craftsmen in a feudal society; proprietors and shareholders as well as doctors and labourers in a capitalist society. This is to say that in any class society there is a social division of labour between exploiters and exploited, in which any technical necessities are of tangential importance. One complication arising from this is that some positions emanating from a division of labour in society carry with them considerable 'power' which we can define for the present as a social practice in which the characteristics of some roles enable their actors to manipulate and control actors in other roles. Another complication is that the power is associated with claims to wealth and privilege at the expense of the rest of society.

Societies then, have positions and occupations with varying degrees and measures of power and wealth, accompanied by differences in privilege. There issues therefore a condition where any one position or occupation is more or less desirable.

Sociologists tend to agree that the attachment of more or less worth to a given position should be called status. Thus any position, in society which attaches worth to the various locations in its structure, will have a high status or a low status and a recognised appropriate complex of claims upon, and duties towards, other statuses in the structure.

The view taken here is that social class is a more fundamental category than status. One element in the class concept is that it refers to those locations in the social structure related to making and distributing goods. Another element is historical. It embraces the fact that culture is cumulative: there is always a material embodiment of past labour, much of which shapes current practices of production and further accumulation.

Any social class is to be recognised by its peculiar mode of access (i) to the material embodiment of past labour and (ii) to the flow of goods from current labour. To put the matter briefly, a social class is to be recognised by its particular position in the economy, where the economy does have a class structure.

We have arrived then at an understanding that power, status and social class are terms which indicate the essential inequalities prevalent in a given society. Without roles enabling the manipulation of persons there would be no 'power'; without differentials in worth attached to positions there would be no 'status'; without differences in access to wealth and income there would be no 'social class'.

Before we elaborated these bases of social inequality we talked of role-change as a process of social movement. Now a new quality is added: movement from one role to another can mean more than merely a change in positions. Movement from role to role carries with it the possibility that a change in status will be involved. This is the special meaning with which is invested the well-known phrase 'social mobility'. Only in a society with social classes and with stratified statuses can there be any possibility of what is implied in social mobility. The notion of joining a group with access to more wealth or greater income than one had before in common with others, or joining a poorer group, can thrive only in a society which has the said inequalities. And the same may be said of status and of power.

There are various modes of existence for the idea of social mobility, not excluding the commandment 'Thou shalt not harbour such a thought'. For example, the caste system of India is frequently cited as an instance where movement from one caste to another is taken to have been impossible. Recruits to Brahmin, Kshatriyah, Vaisya, or Sudra are born into them. There is no other mode of entry. The castes are therefore understood (by modern sociologists) to be self-recruiting—and religious belief supports (in the eyes of the same beholders) that understanding. Ascription could go no further. Yet, for those who believe in Hinduism, there flourishes the impulse towards social mobility by spiritual means. For karma, the sum of actions of an individual's cycle of existences, determines the form of reincarnation and provides a route of social mobility without conflict. More, in the goal of Nirvanah, negation of individual existence, unity with the universal spirit, is expressed the striving for an end to the caste-imposed alienation of human beings from one another.

We should not accept too easily however, any notion that the caste system was always and is now an unchallenged regulation of recruitment to its various strata. The firm establishment of what Weber calls 'the magical distance between castes' appears to have been an outcome of struggle over centuries to substitute for that order of privilege and wealth with its attendant recruitment system, quite another one. In this connection, Engels, in his study of the rise of the Athenian state makes the generalisation that abolition of one form of private property had always been in favour of another form of private property.

In feudal society with its legally defined estates we find another structure where birth, or heredity, constitutes the main recruiting agency to positions of wealth, rank and power. But social mobility here is still possible, mainly through the church which grew over the centuries following the legalisation of Christianity to become itself a part of the economic, status and power structure. Although this route of social ascent is not as free from conflict as the permitted Hindu mode of acceptable mobility over a series of existences, its process is not as productive of violence as the wars between combinations of feudal families or the struggles of the bourgeoisie against the aristocracy or the international imperialist wars waged for trading supremacy.

What is different in the modes of recruitment to positions of domination and privilege in an industrial society as compared with a pre-industrial society is that in the former these positions are not understood to be attributes of birth alone. Access to goods and to power is governed only by their possession as long as this ownership results from actions which break no laws. And since in modern industrial society all are held to be equals before those laws—irrespective of birth—there are no legal inhibitions to social mobility on grounds of class origin.

This is not to say that no advantages accrue from being born into families already in a position of power and with access to wealth. Plainly, in the vast arena of continuous, many-sided, varied and multifarious competitive activities that make up modern economic practice, it is harder for a member of a poor and relatively powerless family to be recruited to a position of control and wealth than for a member of a family already there. However, legal, religious and moral obstructions to such mobility are absent. In fact, social mobility construed as striving to obtain, wealth, power and honour is positively encouraged.

It has been necessary to discuss social movement and social mobility in order to make quite clear the essential characteristic of achievement in respect of social mobility. As has been stated, this is not achievement in the sense of excellent work performance or its recognition. Achievement here is essentially the winning of positions which guarantee wealth and power over persons. Its obverse is escape from positions of poverty and from subjection to the power of other persons.

This is true of both pre-industrial and industrial class societies. In the former however, the thrust generated from the lower orders for social mobility is weak and restricted, whereas in industrial societies the drive for this kind of achievement is urgent, strong, widespread and invested with honour.

Sorokin's theory of social mobility

A general theory of social mobility has been worked out by Pitrim Sorokin in *Social and Cultural Mobility* (1964 edn) which has been referred to by D. V. Glass as 'the only comprehensive work in the field'. For Sorokin every society is stratified occupationally, politically and economically. A profile can be drawn accordingly but climbing, sinking, or lateral movement will be inevitable in 'social space' even though the frequency or intensity of such movement will be different in different societies and at different times. No historical 'trend' is to be found for social mobility, and though 'the removal of the juridical and religious obstacles tended to increase mobility' (p.153) a limit is imposed in modern conditions by wealth.

Channels of social mobility are the army, the church, and education. But schools which are like a 'social elevator' when everyone can go to them, do not run to the top storeys if 'the privileged kind of schools are accessible only to the higher strata'. In the organisations associated with power a variety of political groupings including parties provide ways of advancement. But the most direct upward route is by means of money-making organisations.

Marxism which examines the origins and connections of historically given social classes cannot concur with Sorokin's method which is to position strata in an eternal hierarchy. The inferiority of Sorokin's approach becomes apparent when we take up his treatment of a given class—the proletariat (p.157).

> Since the class of the proletariat is recruited principally from the failures of the upper strata and from the less intelligent elements of the lower classes incapable of ascent, the real significance of such slogans as 'the dictatorship of the proletariat' is evident. With the exception of a small talented section within this class, this means the dictatorship of people who are less intelligent and capable, who are failures, who have defects in health, in character, in mind and who do not have integrity of personality. The inevitable result of such dictatorship is disintegration of a society controlled by such leaders.

Sorokin's book was first published in 1927, when certain hopes were still nourished in capitalist circles concerning the ability of the very first dictatorship of the proletariat to withstand attempts at its destruction. Its second edition was in 1941 when the most élite of élitists states, Nazi Germany, launched its war on the territory of that dictatorship only to find its grave there. Thus history indicates the non-fulfilment of Sorokin's predictions. On the contrary: the politico-military record confirms the relative stability of various forms of the dictatorship of the proletariat; the economic record confirms the viability and integrative possibilities inherent in such societies; the educational record of such dictatorships confirms the possibility of widening educational facilities and of a continuously increasing number of highly educated men and women; the record of health services in such states confirms also the possibility of a homogeneously healthy, purposeful, capable and confident society.

This is valid empirical criticism. On the theoretical side we have to consider Sorokin's simple definition of the proletariat as the class of 'failures'. It may be safely said that this is in no sense a sociological definition. It is the writer's belief that most sociologists would, with Marx, define the proletariat as that class, propertyless in the sense of having no means of production to bring into play for economic ends, which must therefore sell its labour power for wages. They would add that in a capitalist system of productive relations this proletariat is a class of exceptional significance.

But Marxists see also in the proletariat a social class potentially and actually capable of grasping and wielding political power. This is the special insight which no other theoretical standpoint, before the act, could envisage. And in respect of this, it is strange that Sorokin is blind to the logic that when the proletariat establishes its dictatorship it becomes the victorious, the successful class and negates its position of so-called failure. Then the failures are the propertied classes now doomed to disintegration.

Yet another difficulty for the theoretical orientation of those who think like Sorokin is that the successful proletariat retains its propertylessness. There is no redistribution of exclusive, inheritable access to wealth. This exclusive access, better known as private property, is progressively abolished by the economic measures of the proletariat holding political power. Consequently, there is brought into being a society without stratification based upon one or another mode of ownership of the means of production. That is to say there is brought into being a socialist system. If therefore one measures 'success' or 'achievement' by the yardstick of the private acquisiton of capital and sees all social endeavour bent to this purpose, the historic fact of socialism must seem to be a logical impossibility.

And this, of course, is how Sorokin thinks (p.57):

Under normal conditions, free from any social catastrophe, for a society which has passed beyond the primitive stage and is compound in its structure, and maintains the institutions of private property, the fluctuations in the height and the profile of its economic stratification are limited.

A necessary conclusion from this criticism is that the type of social change towards which proletarian class consciousness aspires has little to do with social mobility as defined here. The first is social revolution, the latter is movement from one stratum to another. The first must concern itself with focusing upon and understanding the differences between the proletariat and the bourgeoisie. The second brings members of one social grouping to be on the look-out for personal opportunities to rise from a lower status or to maintain a higher one.

For this reason Marx himself devoted no more than a paragraph in *Capital* to a phenomenon taxing the inventiveness, time and ingenuity of researchers into its ramifications (1926 edn, vol. III, p.587).

> The circumstance that a man without fortune but possessing energy, solidarity, ability and business acumen may become a capitalist in this manner [receipt of credit]—and the commercial value of each individual is pretty accurately estimated under the capitalist mode of production—is greatly admired by the apologists of the capitalist system. Although this circumstance continually brings an unwelcome number of new soldiers of fortune into the field and into competition with the already existing individual capitalists, it also reinforces the supremacy of capital itself, expands its base and enables it to recruit ever new forces out of the substratum of society. In a similar way, the circumstance that the Catholic church in the Middle Ages formed its hierarchy out of the best brains in the land, regardless of their estate, birth or fortune, was one of the principal means of consolidating ecclesiastical rule and suppressing the laity. The more a ruling class is able to assimilate the foremost minds of a ruled class the more stable and dangerous becomes its rule.

When, therefore, in the realms of educational politics, emphasis is laid upon widening opportunities for children of the working class to enter grammar schools, direct grant schools, or public schools, two states of mind are induced: (i) a blindness to the existence and purposes of the bourgeoisie; (ii) a preoccupation with social climbing. More, in the acceptance of better and more educational avenues of social mobility as a valued end, there is involved an acceptance of the capitalist definition of education as it is expressed in the different sorts of schools.

For this reason Marxists reject ease of social mobility as an item of democratic or of socialist policy in education. Instead, it looks towards ending institutionalised privilege in education and towards the development of schools and curricula no longer differentiated by reference to social class or occupational hierarchy.

We must now move on to consider Sorokin's theory of 'spontaneous and natural' origin of social classes. First, with regard to small groups it may be claimed that norms must be met by and are more binding upon the so-called 'leader' than upon any other member. Second, on a larger scale, it can be shown that there are many associations where power remains securely with the collectivity itself and where rules and regulations are designed to ensure that this remains so.

With regard to whole societies, our own experience is, immediately, of a society with a dominant state apparatus functioning on behalf of a ruling capitalist class. Hence it is not an adequate basis upon which to refute or support Sorokin's thesis. However, we are better able to do this than were Marx and Engels in 1847 when they wrote in the *Manifesto of the Communist Party* that 'The history of all hitherto existing society is the history of class struggles'. Some forty years later, Engels, in a footnote, remarked that this statement referred to 'all written history', but that a body of evidence was accumulating to show that societies without class divisions and without state organisations (power structures standing apart from the populace) characterised early 'living together'. Certainly in 1972 the view that there has always been state apparatus is strongly challenged. Thus Eleanor Burke Leacock citing Knader (1968), Fried (1960), Bohannan (1963) and Sahlins (1968) in the Introduction to *Origin of the Family, Private Property and the State* comments (p.48):

> Although anthropologists in the United States have seldom criticised Lowie's theory of state directly, it is no longer of much influence. In keeping with a revived evolutionary perspective, there is a widespread recognition among contemporary anthropologists that the state emerged as a qualitatively new institution associated with marked economic inequalities, a well-developed division of labour, and sizable urban centres.

Once it is accepted that human societies have lived without differences in relationship to means of production and therefore without exploitation and a consequent need for a coercive state organisation, the theory of 'spontaneous and natural' origin of social classes must fall. When he is not intent upon proving this theory Sorokin himself, in this light, chops it down when he writes: 'Beyond doubt the economic pyramid of all primitive societies and of the earliest stages of European, American, Asiatic and African societies has been very low and near to flatness' (1964 edn, p.60). It was in such conditions that 'the kings and chiefs of the greater part of the primitive societies have been elected'. It may be added that they were also subject to deposition, and that the location of power could not have resided, therefore, in the office of chieftainship or kingship as it was then understood.

Since no 'spontaneous' origin of social classes can be proved we can look for an historical origin. It is precisely this historical origin which is explained by Marxism which holds that for an understanding of the most important phenomena in human affairs, the proper starting point is with societies' ways of procuring their food, clothing and shelter. Engels elaborates (1972 edn, p.220. My italics):

The increase in production in all branches—cattle raising, agriculture, domestic handicraft—*gave human labour power the capacity to produce a larger product than was necessary for its maintenance.* At the same time it increased the daily amount of work to be done by each member of the gens, household, community or single family. It was now desirable to bring in new labour forces. War provided them; prisoners of war were turned into slaves.

In the sense that classes arose from human productive relations this origin may be seen to have been a 'natural' one. In the sense that they arose from accumulated knowledge, herds, tools and so on, 'no catastrophic or extraordinary factors' are needed for their appearance. On the other hand, as it is improbable that the forces of production will cease to develop, and as their line of development increasingly requires large scale co-operative effort, it is at least possible that private ownership will have to go, and, with that, planning for social need will take the place of producing for profit. In other words, a sound explanation for the origin of class divisions in society provides at the same time an awareness that their eternal existence is by no means assured. This in turn leads on, possibly, to an understanding of the conditions which must attend their disappearance.

It is because Sorokin's theory of the impossibility of abolishing stratification is as faulty as his theory of its spontaneous and natural appearance that his 'factors' of social mobility explain so little. Leave on one side the issue of whether the existence of social classes must characterise any society, there are still the indisputable facts that some social classes have ceased to exist or have been severely reduced in relative size and in importance, whereas other social classes have come into existence, have grown in size and in significance. On a model in which individuals and groups move up or down, or left or right, quantitative-qualitative change, compositional alteration, appearance and disappearance of social classes, all seem to be beside the point. In place of a theory which knows of an order of progression of different class structures, which examines the history of capitalism, first in its struggle against feudalism, then in full possession of a state apparatus, later in its imperialist heyday, now having to coexist with powerful socialist states whilst strongly waged class struggle proceeds within its frontiers, we are offered a general theory which proclaims: 'Thus in any society at any time there is going on a struggle between the forces of stratification and those of equalisation. The former work permanently and steadily, the latter convulsively, violently, and from time to time' (ibid., p.63). The same theory explains revolution in terms of lag in social mobility.

We come now to a matter of key importance for the sociology of education. From the social perspective, are family and school essentially institutions for testing, selecting and distributing persons with a view to filling positions in the social structure? If the major cause of differences in ability is indeed, as Sorokin claims, genetic endowment, this must be true. From the beginning however, we have stressed learning capacity as a distinctive species-characteristic of human beings. Such a view insists upon the active, formative pressures of family upon its new and growing members, so that children learn, with modifications, to be what their elders were. Families are socialising agencies.

What is wrong with Sorokin's conceptual orientation is that he sees a search being made, by trial and error in the first place, for criteria by which to judge possessors of fit and adequate talents to fill given social positions. And the searcher is society: 'Society had to invent an indirect criterion for discovering and ascertaining the abilities of its members.' Society, however, has no existence outside its institutions, that is outside its families and its non-kinship organisations.

The new recruits to society are the children born into the families it comprises. What the children learn in their families prepares them, trains them, to a degree, for entry into positions corresponding with family expectations and for the inauguration of new families whereby the process will be continued.

But the deepest division between the social classes is that which rests upon ownership of means of production by a few families. Such ownership is inheritable. To the content of socialisation process in the dominant propertied classes must be added therefore, inheritability of private property as a major inducement to class solidarity. These are the two major forces, promoted by the family which ensure loyalty towards and continuity of the values, the attitudes, the appropriate abilities generated by classes in a position of dominance and ownership. There does not exist some sort of embodiment of society as a whole ranging around and conducting experiments in selection.

Upward vertical social mobility from salary and wage-earners of modern Western industrial society, to the capitalist class is effected by a negligible few. The direction of mobility from one status to another in the hierarchy of occupations (though it involves relatively small numbers) is effected by considerably more. But the significance of its very possibility continually demonstrated is twofold. First, it serves to emphasise the experience that, given the continuation of capitalism, there is no economic or other motivation to stay in the working class. Inheritance provides no bond of family or class solidarity in the ranks of the propertyless. Solidarity for them can only be the outcome of awareness of exploitation realised in the continuous presentation of their plight periodically redefined in statements of immediate interests. Such definition is helped by the pursuit also of more ultimate goals. Thus Marx and Engels state that: 'The communists fight for the attainment of the . . . momentary interests of the working class; but in the movement of the present, they also represent and take care of the future of that movement' (1969 edn, p.81).

The second significance of the known and perceived possibility of upward social mobility is the definition that this has provided for educational institutions and educational endeavour. Schools are of great and growing importance in the lives of children born into our modern industrial society. When Sorokin asserts them to be 'primarily testing, selecting and distributing' agencies he is providing a definition which accords with the experience of teachers, parents, pupils, employers and higher educational organisations. That same experience—especially of teachers—makes the definition incomplete. The first kind of purpose served by schools is the teaching to children of what they will need to know and be able to do in order further to acquire the practices relevant to their prospective positions in society. Sorokin points out that some societies have 'privileged kind of schools'. He could have said that all capitalist societies have a hierarchy of schools. Their requirement arises precisely because there is a want by parents with privilege to institutionalise complementary continuation of family socialisation. That want is gratified by the provision of school socialisation of like quality.

Schools available to most wage and salary earners are largely provided by the state—an organisation which, we have indicated, exercises power on behalf of the ruling class. In consequence, the history of British schools manifests a changing definition of education in line with the interests of that class. Socialisation in the state schools, therefore, has been in the direction of weakening the class consciousness and solidarity of the proletariat. The major strategy in continuous operation here is the provision of educational advantage and the promise of occupational reward to those who show willingness to accept the values promoted. The double objective is to convince some children that they are cleverer, that they can manage a richer curriculum, and that they may and ought to, as a result, move up and out of their class of origin, while the rest are persuaded that their limitations entitle them to inferior teaching, an impoverished curriculum, and an occupation of low status.

There is a qualification. This stems from the fact that the capitalist state machine never has its own way entirely with the working class. For example, its battle with the trade unions for nearly two hundred years leaves the unions more permanently secure as organisations than they have ever been. Yet it continues. Similarly, educational policies of capitalism have had to make their compromises with the educational demands coming from the working class.

In this connection it should be understood that by the end of the nineteenth century class consciousness for the British proletariat was being generated at several levels. One level was that of a readiness to organise at the workplace; another was of a conviction that established organisations should be strengthened and developed lest the accumulation of defensive-offensive power be eroded. A third was commitment to political action which would ultimately replace capitalism with socialism. This last moved the dedicated to acquire a more or less sophisticated understanding of the national and international prerequisites for the attainment of working-class power.

At all levels of class consciousness the need for knowledge has always made itself felt, and working-class organisations have tried to cater for this independently. At the same time they have been concerned for the provision of education for working-class children as one more consumer good which could be available in greater or lesser supply, better or worse quality. In contrast here with individual parents' possible aspirations for their own children, the educational aims of the working-class movement had no option but to be oriented to the interests of all children of the working class.

The teachers in the state schools have, in their own way, been motivated by similar purposes. Asher Tropp in *The School Teachers* expresses the belief that 'In part due to the existence of a strong manual trade union movement they could imitate . . . large sections of the English black-coated groups have organised occupationally to achieve their ends and as individuals they are exceptionally active in political life' (1957, p.3).

The sources of the teachers' concern were—as they continue to be—the actualities of capitalism as represented in their pupils, the problems arising from the practice of their vocation, the schools as organisations and their status as teachers in society. Again and again these actualities have pressed them into common cause with the industrial proletariat. Tropp sums up their situation in the 1880s, which, as a pattern, may be regarded as typical (p.149):

> The hostility of a large section of the middle classes towards the elementary teachers and their union, the feeling that the social mobility of the individual teacher had come up against 'caste lines' and the very real frustration the teachers experienced in their work due to the gap between what their training and conscience told them 'could be' and the actual state of the schools—all these were forcing the teachers into co-operation with the radicals and the working class movement.

These are the processes and elements of class consciousness and they show that education—as enlightenment, as the development of mental power, as an ingredient of class betterment—and not upward social mobility has been the demand of the industrial working class and the teachers in the schools for the children. That this is still the case may be seen in the current debates on primary, secondary and higher education.

It is incontestable that schools are seen as institutions where learning and teaching go on—albeit of different kinds in different ways and for different purposes. Moreover, teachers see learning as the cardinal activity they must promote—the conditions of learning their central study. How is it then that social mobility obtains the importance it does in the sociology of education and that Sorokin's elevation of this to the prime reason for the very existence of schools should be plausible?

The answer to this lies in the dynamic totality of capitalism and the attendant purposes of capitalists. As has been shown, industrial societies make continuous changes in labour-power requirements. The direction of these changes is towards a work force with a reducing proportion of hand-workers—especially of the unskilled—and a correspondingly growing proportion of workers 'with qualifications'.

The changing balance of the work force, however, is not seen in the short run, It presents itself to manual workers' children or to the manual workers themselves in the form of 'opportunities'. Thus, what is a matter of necessity to capitalist firms in the shifting ratio of 'staff' to 'hands' and a matter of unavoidable policy for the capitalist class as a whole—expansion of secondary and higher education, besides, more recently, expansion of pre-school education —can be presented as the work of a beneficent state apparatus meeting consensus opinion.

More, a certain criticism of privilege now becomes very useful to the ruling class: criticism of the educational and other advantages enjoyed by professional workers. Shielded by definitions of social class so subtle as to make exploitation seem crude and absurd, the capitalist class have raised little objection to the high-powered 'researchlights' exposing the obstacles—especially the educational obstacles—to upward social mobility, besetting working-class children. The usefulness is on two counts: (i) the means of producing the appropriate skill-and-knowledge organisms in sufficient quantity are suitably expanded and reconstructed; (ii) the more fundamental interests of the working class are left in comparative darkness.

Allowed to flourish too is that other illusion, that the ultimate in educational reform, the provision of true equality of opportunity by application of 'positive discrimination', will dissolve class differences and be the main instrument of introducing a new era cured of its underprivileged. If everyone moves 'up' in the social scale as a consequence of educational betterment, the classless society which, it was claimed, was being inaugurated by affluence in the fifties, will at last be accomplished by education in the eighties, or the nineties, or some time after. And this without the winning of political power by the working class.

But Marxism holds that workers' political power is the indispensable first, necessary prerequisite for a society without exploitation, without classes. Not social mobility but revolution is the necessary inaugurative principle. This is not to say that nothing can be done before working-class power is a fact. The struggle for improvements in the education of working-class children is of this level of importance: without the prosecution of that struggle neither the means of mounting the 'ultimate' offensive nor the ideology to sustain it can take shape and grow. Moreover, any gains secured in educational advance may help in the development of working-class class consciousness as much as it assists the current purposes of finance-capital. The matter has been expressed, though not in class terms, by K. Coates and R. Silburn in *Education for Democracy* (1972, p.61):

> the schools themselves could become to a degree, centres of
> social regeneration: growth points of a new social consciousness
> among the poor, which might bring poverty under attack from
> its sufferers, no less than from the all-too-small battalions of
> liberal welfare-workers and social administrators. . . . Yet . . .
> Education, in itself, will not solve the problem of poverty. The
> social structure that generates poverty generates its own shabby
> education system to serve it; and while it is useful to tackle the
> symptom, the disease will continually find new manifestations
> if it is not understood and remedied. The solution to poverty
> involves, of course, the redistribution of effective social power
> . . . it seems to us that educational provision alone cannot solve
> even the problem of educational poverty, if only because in this
> sphere there are no purely educational problems.

Sponsored and contest mobility

So easy is the acceptance of selection as the main purpose of educational systems that an interesting literature on the subject has flowered. Two of the most esteemed examples of this work are Professor Ralph Turner's essay on contest and sponsored mobility systems (1971) and Earl Hopper's theoretical discussion on educational systems as regulators of ambition (1971).

The major thesis of Turner is that British and American schools reflect the modes of vertical social mobility as they exist in society as a whole. Consequently a sponsorship system operates in British schools overseen by the élite who engage in the educational process to allocate pupils, from their early years, to routes appropriate to their ultimate, rational, occupational roles. But the USA has a contest mobility system—egalitarian because everyone has an equal chance to grasp at the prizes late in the educational process and because the élite are recognised by the masses.

No evidence whatever is advanced to show that in Britain—outside educational institutions—movement from one social class to another, or from one occupational grade to another, is sponsored. Neither is any sponsoring agency outside the schools identified. Some reference there is to a well entrenched bureaucracy, and a suggestion that the logic of the surviving aristocratic system is reflected in the sponsored mobility pattern. However, what we know of aristocracies is that they tend to inhibit rather than sponsor mobility. Moreover it is completely erroneous to imagine that because patterns imported into an established culture tend to be reshaped into coherence with established cultures as they are assimilated that the industrial, commercial and social transformation of Britain from 1750 onwards tolerated anything more than vestiges of aristocratic control two hundred years later. On the contrary, the outcome of capitalist industry and agriculture was the disestablishment of aristocratic cultural norms. The remnants of feudal relationships accommodated themselves to capitalist institutions.

With this in mind we would be better advised to study the differences between the educational systems of Britain and the USA by reference to the overall histories of capitalism in both countries, paying particular attention to the different characteristics of their respective working-class movements.

In Britain it is just short of a century since the working class took irrevocable steps to create its independent political organisations and half a century since its first Labour Prime Minister. The strength of the trade unions, of the Co-operative movement, their support for the Labour Party and through it their own political pressures constitute a major difference with the USA. The political class consciousness of the British working class is ahead of that of the USA and the structure of the education system reflects this as does the wider structure of social security arrangements, grants and so on. Specifically, one has to recognise that the introduction of selection, epitomised in the slogan equality of opportunity, and realised in the provision of educational advantage for the chosen, was in the nature of a compromise between working-class pressure for secondary education for all and changing labour-force requirements in industry. It demonstrated a certain sophistication on the part of the ruling class in its handling of the class struggle.

Thus the welfare state arrangements in Britain have more to do with the history of the labour movement than with vestiges of aristocratic institutions, and those educational concessions which have been made to working-class children are in large measure part of the same story.

Finally for this section of the critique, it should be pointed out that in Britain, teachers, parents and children regard primary schooling as organised competition—that is, a contest—for favoured places in tertiary education. As for America, according to Parsons (1961), the function of the teacher in the elementary school class, that is, early in the lives of the children, is predominantly one that belongs to Turner's sponsorship model. 'Above all', writes Parsons, 'she must be the agent of bringing about and legitimising a differentiation of the school class on an achievement axis' (1961, p.444).

But Turner's thesis offers us something more. He recognises that the mobility function of a private secondary school is quite tangential to it. That being so, something else must be central: the purpose of equipping those who attend them with the knowledge, abilities and attitudes necessary to a ruling capitalist class. What is presented as a minor element in Turner's thesis assumes considerable significance in a Marxist orientation: mobility—i.e. selection—is urged as being central to state supported schools, but is only tangential to schools training the children of the ruling class for their role inheritance.

Why this should be so is also found in Turner's essay. He writes (p.77):

Every society must cope with the problem of maintaining loyalty to its social system. . . . The most conspicuous control problem is that of insuring loyalty in the disadvantaged classes toward a system in which their members receive less than a proportional share of society's goods.

Translated, this formula gives us the following meaning: The capitalist class must seek to maintain the loyalty of the working class to the social system under which it is exploited.

How this is managed is also explained, in part by Turner (p.18).
In a system of contest mobility this [loyalty] is accomplished by
a combination of futuristic orientation, the norm of ambition,
and a general sense of fellowship with the elite. . . . A
futuristic orientation cannot of course be inculcated
successfully in all members of the lower strata but sufficient
internalisation of a norm of ambition tends to leave the
unambitious as individual deviants. . . . Where this kind of
control operates rather effectively it is notable that deviancy is
more likely to take the form of an attack upon the conventional
or moral order than upon the class system itself.

A realistic response to capitalism on the part of all sections of the
working class would be to attack the class system itself. But the
system proposes, through market mechanisms before which we are
all equal, the theoretic possibility of escape from exploitation. The
actual possibility of social mobility—movement from exploited to
exploiter—for the exception, becomes the primary illusion of an
entire class. The education system together with a differential
distribution of rewards according to employment, combine to foster
a secondary illusion. Qualifications obtained in educational institutions become application permits for movement from one section of
the proletariat to another, where exploitation is seen to be less severe
or less onerous.

In Britain too the unambitious and the revolutionary are prone to
be labelled as deviant—as they are in the USA. As for the controls
said by Turner to be typical of sponsored mobility, it would be
surprising if they were found to be absent from the USA. These may
be summarised as, a system training the masses to regard themselves
as relatively incompetent to manage society, by restricting access to
the skills and manners of the élite, and by cultivating belief in the
superior competence of the élite.

Our debt to Professor Turner, therefore, is not for his definition of
two ideal types of social mobility, but for his discussion concerning
the part played by the ideology of social mobility generally speaking,
as control exercised by the ruling class over society as a whole. This
system of ideas and belief arising from the dynamics of capitalism is
a source of illusion among all sections of the working class. It is
fostered by educational policies which adopt equality of opportunity
to become socially mobile, as a dominant ideal.

The regulation of ambition

For Earl Hopper, all societies, no matter how simple, have to solve the problem of the conduct and management of the total selection problem. The hardest part of this is the regulation of the ambition of its personnel. On the one hand ambition has to be warmed up to create real competition for allocation to prestige jobs, on the other hand discontent with failure has to be controlled by cooling it out. Educational systems are shaped by the ways in which they contrive to meet these twin tasks: structurally in accordance with organisational arrangements for selection procedures; ideologically in support of the structure (implementation), and also in justification of selection as such (legitimation).

However, the basic self-evident truths are questionable. M. D. Shipman (1971) concludes from his review of the literature concerning educational arrangements in pre-literate societies that the tendency in simple societies for each member to learn the whole culture, rather than some special part of it, meant that there was little sorting out into adult positions through education. Jules Henry (1970), answering the question, 'Are different groups taught different things?' includes in his reply that, 'Fortes, describing education in Tale society emphasises that the uniformity in education there is due to absence of social stratification'.

A tacit assumption by Hopper is that there is only one kind of ambition—social climbing; an explicit assumption is that society does not have a system of ascribed statuses. Now achievement stands in contrast with ascription in that the former involves effort to win prized roles, whereas the latter requires effort to fulfil customary roles. The complements of achievement are selection and upward mobility: in this light and only in this light, rejection is a complement of ascription and so is non-mobility. If Hopper is correct then all statuses are achieved, everyone is selected. The contention here is that ascription operating through family and school is a major mode of recruitment to social class and to occupational and social statuses of all kinds.

What is proposed in this critique is that ascriptive orientations tend to hold constant—subjectively—a complex of roles and statuses. The corresponding form of ambition is that which seeks to win recognition of high normative performance. Justification or legitimation for rights, rewards, privilege is therefore by appeal to custom and tradition—not by appeal to some variation of rational allocation on the basis of types of skill needed by society.

Achievement—or selection—exists side by side with ascription in many societies but is particularly important in an industrial society with a class system, that is, in a capitalist society. The achievement may be by individuals who move, in the case of status promotion, to one or another level of managership or to the practice of specifically valuable skills. In such cases the selection agents are easily recognisable as capitalists or their representatives. It may be of a kind where certain qualifications lead on to a professional occupational status. Here the selection agents are recognisable as agents of the capitalist class when ideological orientations and class connections are analysed. The achievement may be in the nature of class promotion as a consequence of directly capitalistic activities with an expanding basis of exploitation. In this case it is a matter of self-selection by entry into the market as a buyer and not as a seller of labour-power.

Mobility is always tangled up with problems of loyalty. In the first case, for instance, it is evident that the achiever has decided that his immediate, particularistic (personal-familial) interests depend upon universalistic loyalty to the firm. But as an employee, the two sets of interests are not in fact congruent with each other: and his likely rejection of universalistic loyalty to the working class does nothing to remove the antagonism between employee and employer. In the second case, depending on the specific profession, selection is likely to depend upon readiness to subscribe to an altruistic universalism defined in a professional ideal. Capitalist society makes this likely to accompany a decision that particularistic interests are served best by universalistic loyalties to the established class and status structure. Here, not only does an antagonism between employer and employee persist, but conflict is likely to arise between professional and establishment goals. In the third case the realities of market forces impose their own brand of universalism: but here the personal-familial-particularistic loyalties are pursued directly. Selection is of oneself, and validated by market forces and followed by selection of others by the same self. Meanwhile family (in so far as they are not rejected by the property-owner during his lifetime or in his will) are bound particularistically to the same universalistic pressures.

One outcome of this analysis is that there is a type of ambition common to all three cases. This is the ambition to stand in a superior and advantageous position relative to others, the superiority and advantage being represented in greater possessions and in greater command over services.

A second outcome is that the opposition of particularism and universalism is not necessarily an antagonistic one. Antagonisms in the first two cases are seen to disappear in the third. For the bourgeoisie personal-familial loyalty is fostered by the pursuit of universalistic interests and vice versa. This immediately brings to the fore the possibility of generalising the non-antagonistic opposition between personal-familial and universal interests. But for this the necessary prerequisite is the absence of classes and of hierarchial statuses.

A third is that there are two modes of ambition not necessarily associated with that already defined. There is an ascriptive ambition to win recognition of high normative performance. There is an altruistic ambition which is universalistic in that it measures one's own accomplishment by what it achieves for other members of society without reference to subsequent personal advantage.

Although these modes of ambition are found in association with social climbing, the association is frequently an antagonistic one. Moreover, they are, in class societies, generally assumed to have subordinate importance. Given a society in which the complex of roles and statuses has nothing to do with class and little to do with rank (classes and statuses no longer having existence) there emerges the theoretical possibility of the continuous generation of (i) altruistic ambition as a dominant motivation and (ii) high performance ambition in occupational and other roles.

But the essential criticism to be made of the Hopper thesis is that it assumes capitalism and its values to be eternal. The models relating to the control of ambition as a motor of social mobility hinge on the modification of educational systems in such a way as to reduce various types of anxiety resulting from the selection processes themselves. The selection is for statuses which constitute a labour market and the educational systems are each without exception a series of levels of entry—reached by different routes—to this market. The entire theory, then, serves enquiry into control of a certain kind of ambition: ambition to achieve a relatively high value according to criteria applied by the hiring side on the labour market. The objective is to reduce disappointment with possible outcomes of this endeavour.

We may now leave the theoretical enquiry into pathological effects of social climbing and their possible abatement for a Marxist perspective on educational systems.

Social revolution and education

Marx's famous eleventh thesis on Feuerbach 'The philosophers have only interpreted the world, in various ways; the point, however, is to change it' (1969 edn, p.286) applies with great force to education and theorising about educational systems. His third thesis makes this abundantly clear (p.284):

> The materialist doctrine that men are products of circumstances and upbringing and that, therefore, changed men are the products of other circumstances and changed upbringing, forgets that it is men that change circumstances and that the educator himself needs educating. Hence this doctrine necessarily arrives at dividing society into two parts, of which one is superior to society (in Robert Owen, for example).
>
> The coincidence of the changing of circumstances and of human activity can be conceived and rationally understood only as revolutionary practice.

A sociological perspective following this advice will need no apology, therefore, for an attempt to discover meanings and purposes in education which stand in opposition to those derived from and imposed by capitalist ideology. There are, however, two conditions which must be met to secure theoretical worth: (i) that these meanings and purposes be at least discernible during capitalism's own existence—just as socialised production and the proletariat herald social ownership and the abolition of private property; (ii) that the ideas and practices characteristic of capitalism, which inevitably accompany new purposes and meanings during socialism's early stages—especially whilst capitalism is a major force in the world—be shown to be dispensable and transient.

Opposed to the standpoint that education has no way of being anything other than a machinery for training, grading and inducting pupils among existing social and occupational strata including the buyers and sellers on the labour market, is set another. This is the revolutionary standpoint that capitalism generates the necessity for the final abolition of social classes and that socialism generates the necessity for an end to the stratification of occupations. The indicated corresponding transformation in educational systems is from a hierarchical structure of schools, each with its own hierarchy of streams or other selection apparatus, the whole governing access to an order of quality of life chances—into a complex of educational institutions offering a common general course for all children together with arrangements for the development of special interests and facilities for study at different levels at any age, the whole comprising enablement for the maintenance of a homogeneously high quality of living.

This is not to encourage any notion that Marxism proposes the introduction of an egalitarian utopia with an education system to match. Marx's *Critique of the Gotha Programme* is particularly well-known for his forecast of the necessary stages of transition from capitalism—once working-class power is established—to communism. The stages, merging one into the other, are labelled, the dictatorship of the proletariat, socialism, communism. In making this forecast certain other views relevant to a sociology of education are expounded.

Criticising the Lassallean elements of the Programme, he points out that before any distribution of the total social product, there must first be deducted provision for replacement of the means of production . . . for the expansion of production . . . for reserves or insurance. . . . There has to be also a deduction for the satisfaction of needs such as schools, health services, etc. This latter deduction grows in comparison with present-day society and it grows in proportion as the new society develops. The perspective is therefore of expansion in education unhampered by economic interests to the contrary.

With reference to the distribution of what is, after that, a diminished product, Marx points out: (i) that what the producer is deprived of in his capacity as a private individual benefits him directly or indirectly in his capacity as a member of society, (ii) that within the co-operative society based on common ownership of the means of production the producers do not exchange their products. There is therefore no occasion to value products by reference to individual labour content. There is then no market, properly speaking, whether for goods or for labour.

But in the early stages of a socialism in every respect, economically, morally, and intellectually, still stamped with the birthmarks of the old society, the individual producer receives back from society—after the deductions are made—exactly what he gives to it. The relationships of exploitation have gone: now only labour can be given to the productive process and only consumer goods can be obtained. Nevertheless, the bourgeois limitation of equal right remains (1968 edn, vol. II, p.564).

the equality consists in the fact that measurement is made with an equal standard, labour. . . . But one man is superior to another physically or mentally and so supplies more labour in the same time, or can labour for a longer time. . . . This equal right is an unequal right for unequal labour. It recognises no class differences, because everyone is only a worker like everyone else; but it tacitly recognises unequal individual endowment and thus productive capacity as natural privilege. . . . Further, one worker is married, another not; one has more children than another and so forth. Thus with an equal output and hence an equal share in the social consumption fund, one will in fact be richer than another and so on.

This basic inequality during the first stages of a socialist society arises from the continuation, obsolescent though it may be, of a bourgeois norm: the legitimation of natural privilege by applying the rule of equal right, by restricting its application to a specific area of human activity, in the case under discussion, the right to sustenance measured by work contributed (ibid.).

It is therefore a right of inequality in content like every other right. Right, by its very nature can only consist in the application of an equal standard; but unequal individuals . . . are measurable by an equal standard in so far as they are brought under an equal point of view, are taken from one definite side only, e.g. in the present case are regarded only as workers and nothing more seen in them; everything else ignored.

The contention here is that the socialist framework sketched by Marx has been realised in the Soviet Union, and in a number of other countries where an end has been put to private ownership of the means of production and of a social class structure based on such ownership. What shortfalls there are from the target of a communist society match the projections made concerning the influence of capitalist norms on what was for Marx the socialist future. In the realisation of that socialist framework the feasibility of a developed communist society is however established. Marx saw this in the following terms (p.556).

In the higher phase of communist society, after the enslaving subordination of individuals under a division of labour, and therewith also the antithesis between mental and physical labour, has vanished, after labour has become not merely a means to live but has become itself the prime necessity of life, after the productive forces have also increased with the all-round development of the individual, and all the springs of co-operative wealth flow more abundantly—only then can the narrow horizon of bourgeois right be fully left behind and society inscribe on its banners: from each according to his ability, to each according to his needs.

Now it cannot be expected that the characteristics of a communist society will reveal themselves fully where the first historic steps are yet to be taken. Nevertheless, the problems afflicting capitalism in a world where the transition towards socialism has already begun indicates also their solutions. These indications are all the stronger for the fact that social revolution has been staved off in the most advanced centres only to burst forth in their backyards—in the countries subjected to the most intense exploitation that is, where the fetters of productive relations have placed the most severe constrictions upon the productive forces.

Socio-economic pressures have not abated with the evasion of social revolution. The requirements of technological (forces of production) development are for an educational system wherein all-round general education is provided at a relatively high level for an increasing proportion of its flow of recruits. Since the rate of change is so rapid, narrow vocational training is having to give way to an education which makes for flexibility. This is to say that a modern educational ideal accepts the objective of ending the enslaving subordination of individuals under a division of labour. Again, unskilled manual workers are not in such great demand and are diminished both as a proportion of the labour force and in absolute numbers. This, taken together with the need for more skilled workers, the skill itself changing from a manipulative to a cognitive basis, points to technological pressure for ending the antithesis between mental and physical labour.

In this connection the views of Professor Jerome Bruner (*The Times Educational Supplement*, 27 October 1972) concerning a good fit of educational aims with the dynamics of modern industrial society are highly significant. Because 'the most evolved organisation of intentions is vocation or profession or career organised work' because 'the decision to delay vocational or job decision until comparatively late in life inevitably makes fuzzy one's definition of oneself as an adult', he proposes that, 'the first order of business in the transformation of our mode of education is to revolutionise and revivify the idea of vocation or occupation.' The motor of this transformation should be the conception of the process of education 'as a form of enablement selectively available throughout the life cycle'.

Professor Bruner reminds us that there is an 'extreme . . . where the structure of one's life and one's work are indistinguishable'. What we know also is that there exists, even under capitalism, a gathering momentum of demand for this kind of identification. We have thus discovered a pronounced pressure for an order wherein 'labour has become not merely a means to live but . . . the prime necessity of life'.

In capitalist society the relations of production and the super-structure of ideology, law and government hold back the political changes that could properly release the educational energies making for the kinds of change outlined. Concern is, by implication, for the retention of the class and status systems, where progress is defined in terms of precision of selection and ease of social mobility. To discover whether the norms in a socialist society operate in another way it is possible—and necessary because it is possible—to look at education in the USSR.

Nigel Grant in *Soviet Education* (1965) says that 'its special character' lies in that 'it has always been a mass system and a planned system subject to political control and closely supervised' (p.27). The reason given for the political control is that (p.22),

From the Soviet standpoint the basic issue is quite simple . . .
that education must function according to the needs of society
and that theirs is by definition a socialist society moving towards
communism, a society which needs trained citizens who will be
able—and willing—to continue with the job of social transformation.

The same rationale lies behind its being a mass system. For this social perspective 'would be unattainable if education were regarded as an obstacle race or a sieve for catching the most able and dis-carding the rest' (p.27). A parallel line of reasoning is that mass education solves technological problems. 'A highly selective system might conceivably produce the required intelligensia and specialists though even this is doubtful—in an industrial society . . . education has to raise the entire population to as high a level as possible or the training of specialists is bound to prove futile in practice' (ibid.).

Mass education is practised because the way to communism requires 'positive political commitment among the masses' (p.28). The mass character is insisted upon to such an extent that Grant explains (ibid.):

Reforms may bring in more diverse courses for senior pupils, special schools may cater for artists and ballet dancers, but underlying the variations is the stress on providing a basic general education, covering the same ground and on the same terms for all, regardless of background or future occupation.

It is noteworthy that one aspect of mass education is that policy is directed towards making Soviet schools completely comprehensive (pp.41–2).

Officially, every school of general education caters for an entire age group, regardless of intelligence or attainment, of the area which it serves. . . . Not only does the Soviet system reject the segregation of pupils into grammar-school-type and secondary-modern-type courses, but rejects any kind of segregation within the school. . . . In the USSR all children are given the extensive course in the sciences . . . all learn one foreign language, all go through the same course in history, geography, Russian and so on.

Even those who are hostile to the overall political and social aims of the Soviet Union accept the firmness and vigour of its faith in the educability of all children. Thus, Robert M. Hutchins remarks in *The Learning Society* (1970, p.22):

Whatever may be said of the limitations of Soviet Education, the Russian experience is now long enough for us to say one thing unequivocally about it: it has knocked on the head the notion that only a few can understand difficult subjects. The compulsory eight-year-school established by law in 1959 demands that all pupils learn, between the ages of seven and fifteen, the elements of mathematics, physical and biological science and at least one foreign language . . . reports of disinterested or even hostile observers leave little doubt that, according to Western standards the instruction in these subjects has succeeded.

Hutchins goes on to 'remember where the Soviet Union started', with only a thin layer of 'middle class', a high level of illiteracy and so on, though he makes no mention of the interventionist wars and of the destruction of the Second World War. There is no reference at all to the immense release of educational power derived from the abolition of exploitation. But the contrast between capitalist and socialist educational endeavour becomes quite apparent when he pleads for the USA to learn from the Soviet Union and to reap even greater benefits (ibid., p.23).

All we have to do to appreciate what the Soviet Union has done is to imagine the reponse if it were proposed to introduce the same programme among the Bantus of Africa or even among the Negroes of Harlem or Mississippi. A judgement on the accomplishment of the Communist Chinese is premature; but there is every indication that . . . they too will offer evidence that everybody has the capacity to learn to use his mind.

The concern for a principle that an entire society should move with consciousness and deliberation on the part of the majority—and a growing majority—of its people towards a qualitatively new era is epitomised in the structure of school and family relationships (Grant, 1965, p.58).

Every class has its parents' meetings . . . [which] will meet as a group once or twice every term. . . . At the first of these meetings the parents elect three . . . to serve on the Parents' Committee of the whole school.

The school Parents' Committee is a more elaborate and formal organisation, operating according to instructions from the Minister of Education on composition, activities and procedures. It elects a praesidium of eight . . . elects a chairman who is co-opted to the Pedagogic Council, which consists of the entire teaching staff of the school under the chairmanship of the director.

Here is a system which at the least operates in the direction of reducing the alienation that can be shown to accompany the upward social mobility preoccupation fostered in capitalist cultures. Behaviours reminiscent of such cultures persist in progress-hungry and unco-operative Soviet parents: 'Pushing parents are probably commoner than stubborn ones, but both appear to be in a minority and all the social pressures at the present time are likely to make these minorities still smaller' (p.61).

Writers in the sociology of education commonly point to three major agencies of socialisation: the family, the school, the peer group. We have shown that family and school in the Soviet Union interrelate in such a way as to promote conditions where—given the technological advance confidently expected—status differences between occupations will become decreasingly significant. What is the evidence concerning peer group relationships?

A most thorough-going analysis of how peer groups work in the USSR is made by Urie Bronfenbrenner in *Two Worlds of Childhood* (1972). Outstandingly important is that peer groups are assigned as principal agencies of the society for the upbringing of children. Such primary responsibility is vested in the children's collective defined as 'a group of children united in common, goal-oriented activity and the communal organisation of this activity . . . such collectives constitute the basic structural units in all Soviet programmes designed for the care or education of children' (p.21). From the very earliest age upbringers in nurseries deliberately foster co-operation (ibid.).

Nor is such co-operation left to chance. From the very beginning stress is placed on teaching children to share and to engage in joint activity. Frequent reference is made to common ownership: 'Moe eto nashe; nashe moe' (mine is ours; ours is mine). Collective play is emphasised. Not only group games but special complex toys are designed which require the co-operation of two or three children to make them work. . . . As soon as children are able to express themselves they are given training in evaluating and criticising each other's behaviour from the point of view of the group. Gradually, the adult begins to withdraw from the role of leader or co-ordinator in order to forge a self reliant collective.

The children's collective finds a base in the school class, in accordance with Malarenko whose approach 'places major emphasis on work, group competitiveness and collective discipline' (p.49). Peer groups are brought into positive association with the school and family. They enter into socialist competition between links (rows) in classrooms, between schools and, on a wider scale, between cities and regions. The socialist competition provided a motivation for the whole group to secure adequate performance from each member of the collective and brings each group to find the best ways of helping inadequate members. In this system the children's collective becomes the agent of adult society and the major source of reward and punishment.

Of considerable relevance to the theme of social mobility is Bronfenbrenner's observation that (pp.50–1),

An especially prominent feature of collective upbringing is the emphasis on altruistic behaviour both at the individual and the social level. Not only are the members of the collective taught to help each other, but through the system of . . . group adoption each class takes on responsibility for the upbringing of a group of children at a lower grade level . . . the manner in which they fulfil this civic responsibility enters into the evaluation of their total school performance.

It is Bronfenbrenner's judgment that communal upbringing and education are no passing phase in the USSR (p.90):

whatever the future may hold we have every reason to expect that Soviet society will continue to rely heavily on communal facilities for the care and education of children. And in all of these institutions as well as in the regular schools, the well-proven technique of collective upbringing even if applied with greater tolerance for individual needs will continue to be used.

There emerge from the discussion on Marx's own forecasts, on current problems in advanced capitalist countries and on socialisation processes in the Soviet Union the following propositions:

(1) that the forecasts are in general correct concerning certain basic differences between the motivating influences in socialising agencies—especially schools—in socialist and capitalist societies;

(2) that a modification is required in view of the delayed initiatory political revolution in advanced capitalist societies: education as one element among the forces of production is brought into sharper and increasingly sharper antagonism with the hierarchy of occupations that characterises capitalism;

(3) that initial success of working-class power in countries less advanced (at first) industrially, places considerable weight on new-style socialising agencies—e.g. upbringers to become generating sources of a communist ethic.

The new meanings and objectives in their main outlines are becoming clear. They are to be discerned struggling in capitalist societies against a dominant ideology which elevates personal ambition to first place in an order of values. They are to be seen thriving vigorously in the socialist sector—though still accompanied by obsolescent attitudes and practices—and promoting to that place personal fulfilment through the betterment of one's offering to the collective.

Chapter 5

Social class and education

In search of definitions

The chapter on social mobility has indicated the need to distinguish between occupational grades and social class. It has also tried to show that the competition for occupational status, engendered as it is by the dominant social class, cannot be ended without abolition of classes in the first place. To understand its place in education more fully we must therefore investigate the problem of social class more directly.

Discussion on social class tends, generally, to awaken a kind of cautious prejudice because achievement orientations, political dispositions, and ideological set—all forms of social consciousness—are immediately wakened. No one can be completely free from interest, completely value-free, in this matter because no one is without group membership. And, as Karl Mannheim points out (Petras and Curtis, 1970, p.112),

> The living forces, actual attitudes underlying the theoretical ones . . . have not their origin . . . in the individual's becoming aware of his interests in the course of his thinking. Rather they arise out of the collective purposes of the group, which underlie the thought of the individual and in the prescribed outlook of which he merely participates.

These considerations should not prevent us from coming to grips with the realities expressed in concepts of social class. They should, however, enable us to see that ideology is as active in a perspective which omits class from a statement of educational determinants as it is in one which insists upon it.

Similarly there is no absence of ideological elements in statements to the effect that no social classes exist in Britain, or Western Europe, or America these days, that Marxism and ideas of social class anta-gonism were perhaps relevant to the nineteenth century, or between two World Wars, but that such notions are no longer valid. That social blindness, induced by willingness to serve capitalist purposes, seems to have been as prevalent when Marx and Engels were giving sight to an international working class, weaker then than it is now. Marx, in a letter to Joseph Weydemeyer, in 1852, points out that the most gifted theoreticians of capitalism accepted the existence both of classes and of class struggle (1969 edn, pp.494–5):

He [C. H. Carey] reproaches not only [Ricardo] but Malthus, Mill, Say, Torrens, Wakefield, McCulloch, Senior, Whately, R. Jones, and others, the masterminds among the economists of Europe, with rending society asunder and preparing civil war because they show that the economic bases of the different classes are bound to give rise to a necessary and ever growing antagonism among them. He tried to refute them . . . by attempting to make out that economic conditions—rent (landed property), profit (capital), and wages (wage labour), instead of being conditions of struggle and antagonism, are rather conditions of association and harmony. . . . Long before me bourgeois historians had described the historical development of this class struggle. . . . Ignorant louts like Heinzen, who deny not merely the class struggle but even the existence of classes, only prove that, despite all their bloodcurdling yelps and the humanitarian airs they give themselves, they regard the social conditions under which the bourgeoisie rules as the final product, the *non plus ultra* of history and that they are only the servitors of the bourgeoisie.

And thirty-five years later, Engels had to write in a preface to *The Conditions of the Working Class in England in 1844* the following observation: 'In February 1885, the American public opinion was almost unanimous on this one point: that there was no working class in the European sense of the word, in America.' (1969 edn, pp.526–7.)

Very widespread today is a view of social class which manages to combine configuration with apparent analysis by using the term stratification. What is achieved in the use of a geological analogy is more than figurative speech. Here the existence of social classes and their importance is allowed, but the permanence of the relationship between them is resoundingly asserted. If it is true that the phrase social structure tends to fix for us a complex of ongoing relationships which in their movement must generate change, the expression 'stratification' uses an image conductive to the supposition that the class structure is unalterable by man.

The kind of thinking that goes with the image of stratification is manifested in that which labels the different strata as upper-upper class, upper class, lower-upper class, upper-middle class, middle class . . . and so on down to lower-lower class. Having made the labels the problem then is to say what groups each stratum will comprise and what criteria will be used in making the assignations. It is quite plain that a class analysis of, say, a Greek city state would be very complex, but it could, no doubt, be squeezed one way or another into the labelling system indicated above. (See Rex, *Key Problems in Sociological Theory* (1961) for a summary and explanation of Lloyd Warner's scheme of social stratification.) However, such a labelling system—such a classification—of the social classes to be discovered in the city state would tell us very little about that form of social organisation. The term 'slave' does far more for us than the term 'lower-lower class'. The former immediately conjures up a network of ideas connected with economic, legal, political and other social institutions and interests—ideas immediately contributing to our understanding of Greek social relationships. The latter term, tells us, not only nothing of the sort, but, in the apparent applicability of the same classificatory scheme to a variety of social systems, neglects essential differences between them, and obscures the possibility and the grounds for action to end, once and for all, class exploitation.

The labelling of social classes in modern Britain, especially when educational matters are under investigation usually follows the Registrar General's index.

Social Class I Managerial
II Intermediate
III Skilled Manual Workers
IV Semi-skilled Manual Workers
V Unskilled Manual Workers

Greater precision may be claimed for the Moser-Hall index which subdivides the first two classes of the Registrar General's index into four categories, thus giving,

Social Class I Professional
      II Managerial
     III Supervisory (Higher)
     IV Supervisory (Lower)
      V Skilled Manual Workers
     VI Semi-skilled Workers
    VII Unskilled Manual Workers

These frameworks for organising our understanding of social class in Britain have in common that they do not adequately reveal the class interests at work in our society, and yield explanations of educational phenomena largely conducive to maintaining social relations as they are. It has been pointed out that what is omitted from, is as significant as what is included in a presentation of data. But there are occasions when data generally left out must perforce find a place. Thus when the Royal Commission Report on Industrial Relations was being prepared, research yielded and used the table of social classes (Table 2).

TABLE 2   *Social classes*

	% 1961
1 Employers and proprietors	4·7
2 All white collar workers	35·9
(a) Managers and administrators	5·4
(b) Higher professionals	3·0
(c) Lower professionals and technicians	6·0
(d) Foremen and inspectors	2·9
(e) Clerks	12·7
(f) Salesmen and shop assistants	5·9
3 All manual workers	59·3

It will be seen that all the strata referred to in both the Registrar General's index and that of Moser-Hall have in common that they are employees of the first group: Employers and proprietors.

What needs to be grasped is that modern Britain is a capitalist society with a ruling capitalist class and that indices commonly used to examine educational matters obscure this fact. Reinforcing this deceit is the prevailing use of 'middle class' for every value, attitude and practice seen to be uncharacteristic of manual workers. P. W.

Musgrave, for example, substantiating his important proposition that the definition of education at any time provides evidence of the strains, conflicts and compromises of that society and of that period makes this observation (1968b, p.61):

> The middle class defined the education of the working class as a necessary free service in a minimal form. . . . It must have a curriculum sufficient to ensure a meagre literacy and be suited solely to the lower classes—hence, in an elitist age, it must be entirely unconnected with the ruling class.

Now by 'middle class' in the nineteenth century was understood 'capitalist class' or 'bourgeoisie', whereas by middle class these days is understood members of a broad range of occupations including especially professional employees. It is true, of course, that during the nineteenth century the education of working-class children was defined by the capitalist class. But the substitution of 'middle' (with stratification model in mind) for 'capitalist' (with a bundle of modes of action and of interests in mind) leads on to use of the term 'elitist age' instead of 'laissez-faire capitalist society' and expels, in this way, from the situation, meanings without which that situation cannot be properly understood.

The view of class taken here as being fundamental is the Marxist view. It is an objection by some that Marx gave no definition of social class that could be accepted as being academically adequate. Isaiah Berlin, for example states that (1963, p.8):

> Marx had identified the rising class of his own time with the proletariat, devoted the rest of his life to planning victory for those at whose head he placed himself. . . . [His] sole business is to defeat the enemy. . . . Hence the almost complete absence in Marx's later works of discussion of ultimate principle.

A statement like this may be relevant—apparently—but it ignores the entire methodological stand of Marx. Others complain that Marx left incomplete the famous chapter LII of *Capital*'s third volume wherein he begins to study the three great classes of capitalist society—landowners, capitalists and proletarians—as if in consequence we had been bereft of Marx's analysis of these classes and their patterns of interaction. Engels tells us quite clearly in the preface why the chapter was unfinished and indicates that its nature was to have been to summarise analyses which had constituted the life's work of the author of *Capital* (1926 edn, p.7. My italics).

Lastly, the seventh part was available complete, but only as a

first draft. . . . There exists only the beginning of the final
chapter. It was to treat of the three major classes of developed
capitalist society—the landowners, capitalists and wage-
labourers—corresponding to the three great forms of revenue,
ground-rent, profit, and wages, and the class struggle, an
inevitable concomitant of their existence, as the actual
consequence of the capitalist period. Marx used to leave *such
concluding summaries* until the final editing, just before going to
press, when the latest historical developments furnished him
with unfailing regularity with proofs of the most laudable
timeliness for his theoretical propositions.

The thought and views of Marx in regard to social classes are to
be found in his descriptions and labelling of them: (i) in his accounts
of the complementary and antagonisms of their interactions; (ii) in
analyses of their origins, developments and historic roles; (iii) in
discussions of their strategies during bitter political and social
struggles current in his lifetime. Terms like 'middle', 'lower', 'upper',
abound in the texts but never are they allowed to take on the nature
of a framework within which their essential characteristics may be
hidden.

As we have seen, Marx at no time considered himself as the dis-
coverer of social classes or even of class struggle. He defines clearly
his own part in the matter in his letter to Weydemeyer (1969 edn,
p.494):

And now as to myself, no credit is due to me for discovering
the existence of classes in modern society of the struggle
between them. Long before me bourgeois historians had
described the historical development of this class struggle and
bourgeois economists the economic anatomy of the classes.
What I did was to prove: (i) that *the existence of classes* is only
bound up with *particular historical phases in the development of
production*, (ii) that the class struggle necessarily leads to the
dictatorship of the proletariat, (iii) that this dictatorship itself
constitutes only the transition to the *abolition of all classes* and
to a *classless society*.

The entire work of *Capital* is about the bourgeoisie and the
proletariat, their terms of existence, their motivations and functions
as classes— not to mention the kind of dynamic generated from their
interaction and imparted to society as a whole.

The reason given in the *Communist Manifesto* by Marx and

Engels (1948 edn, pp.21–4) for the closest study of these two classes provides at the same time a list of classes in capitalist societies. 'Of all the classes that stand face to face with the bourgeoisie today, the proletariat alone is a really revolutionary class. The other classes decay and finally disappear in the face of modern industry: the proletariat is its special and essential product'. The bourgeoisie comprise not only that group extruded by the process whereby 'modern industry has converted the little workshop of the patriarchal master into the great factory of the industrialist capitalist'. The appropriation of surplus value—wealth over and above what is expended in labour and other costs—goes on outside as well as inside the factory. 'No sooner is the exploitation of the labourer by the manufacturer so far at an end that he receives his cash, than he is set upon by the other portions of the bourgeoisie, the landlord, the shopkeeper, the pawnbroker etc.

Not that the bourgeoisie and the proletariat are the only classes in capitalist society:

The former lower strata of the middle class—the small
manufacturers, traders and persons living on small incomes, the
handicraftsman and peasants—all these sink gradually into the
proletariat, partly because their diminutive capital does not
suffice for the scale on which modern industry is carried on and
is swamped in the competition with large capitalists, partly
because their special skill is rendered worthless by new methods
of production. Thus the proletariat is recruited from all classes
of the population.

There is also 'The "dangerous class", the social scum, that passively rotting mass thrown off by the lowest layers of the old society' which may participate in a proletarian revolution but which is more likely to play 'the part of a bribed tool of reactionary intrigue'.

It is from *The Eighteenth Brumaire of Louis Bonaparte* where Marx explains the political representation of the French peasantry by the Emperor, that there is inferred a definition of social class with two aspects. After discussing the economic and social terms of existence of the peasant family in France, Marx comments (1969 edn, p.378):

In so far as millions of families live under economic conditions
of existence that separate their mode of life, their interests, and
their culture from those of the other classes, and put them into
hostile opposition to the latter, they form a class. In so far as

there is merely a local interconnection among these small-holding peasants and the identity of their interests begets no community, no national bond, and no political organisation among them, they do not form a class. They are consequently incapable of enforcing their class interest in their own name.

A social class then, is identified, objectively, by the 'economic conditions of its existence' from which flow its life style and the elements of its subculture. Not only is one class to be distinguished from another by these criteria, but their essential modes of inter-action are thereby defined. Since the existence of social classes presupposes the practice of exploitation an underlying antagonism of interest must persist.

On the subjective side a social class is recognised by its class consciousness. This is seen in its ability to act at one level or another in its own interest. In turn, this demands that it should understand its own interest and the strategy necessary for its achievement. A requirement for the appearance of class consciousness is that its objective conditions of existence should be continuously and even increasingly reproduced. This means that pressure for the ends of one class inevitably serves to define the interests of the opposing class. Given this continuity and conflict, class consciousness, which can reside only in the heads of the members of social classes, may be institutionalised in the development of organised class action. The class consciousness of a social class is therefore to be recognised in its economic organisations, its political parties and its literature.

Class consciousness may be more or less widespread and its quality measured by the scope and definition of its long-term and short-term ends. The process of economic history engenders the growth and potency of one social class, the reduction and uselessness of another. For that reason political and intellectual action to support the purposes of the redundant class is reactionary. Similar action for the ends of the rising class is progressive and, at a certain level, revolutionary.

Action is revolutionary when it proceeds from a level of conscious-ness which envisages the transfer of power from one class to another and when the action is oriented to that end. A revolutionary situ-ation is where this transfer becomes possible. Revolutions are historically necessary because nothing can prevent, ultimately, either the historical process or its culmination in a class struggle for political and social power. The outcome of a particular revolutionary situation, however, depends upon the extent and the quality of class consciousness of the contending classes.

The proletariat, the bourgeoisie and education

Capitalism makes the proletariat the revolutionary class. At the same time it makes it the class whose conquest of power must, because it is a propertyless class, usher in the classless society. The economic conditions of existence of the working class are that its members:

(1) possess no important means of production;

(2) must offer for sale their power to work;

(3) are paid wages, the values of commodities necessary to replace that labour-power;

(4) are alienated from that part of their created product which is over and above the value of their labour-power and other means of production;

(5) find themselves in continuous antagonism with their employers over their conditions of labour and their share in the total product.

The bourgeoisie have as their condition of existence that they:

(1) own the most important means of production;

(2) must hire labour to operate these means of production;

(3) advance capital in the form of wages, which is returned to them in the form of commodities;

(4) appropriate surplus value, that is the new value created in excess of the capital invested as wages;

(5) find themselves in continuous antagonism with their employees over conditions of labour and their share in total product.

It is therefore at the point of production where the initial act of exploitation of the working class by the capitalist class occurs.

What has this Marxian conception to do with education? In the first place it concerns education as something worth having for the enrichment—intellectually, aesthetically, socially and physically—of the person who has it. From the class standpoint, education, in this sense, has been regarded as a cumulative experience—especially childhood experience—of a certain kind.

When, therefore, a given quality and length of education is taken by the capitalist class as a right appropriately due to their children and another, shorter, education is made available to the working class, education is understood by both classes to express the relationship of exploitation as palpably as different housing conditions. But the outcome of having or not having access to a certain cultural heritage supports a norm vital to the interaction of exploitation. The superiority of the well-educated over the ill-educated is understood as a comparison between innately superior and inferior human beings—very largely on both sides. The exploitation presents itself as a natural relationship between leaders and followers. The ruling, exploiting class is seen to be the élite, the working class as the masses. This is one reason why educational demands have always been part of any working class overall programme of social objectives. And it is why attacks on educational privilege have always been resisted by the bourgeoisie.

There has been a shift from the grounding of a claim to superior educational facilities on the bare fact of being the capitalist class. This claim is now more generally justified by reference to the intelligence with which the children of the different social classes have been endowed. The Taunton Commission of 1868 made no pretence about the class structure of education. It recognised one class of 'men with considerable income independent of their own exertions' whose children's education at public school went on till eighteen or nineteen, or whose plans for their sons required finishing with school at sixteen. The children of the latter could go then to the same school as those of another class who has to begin earning at sixteen. Then there was a class of farmers, tradesmen and superior artisans whose children finished education at fourteen.

A fourth grade of education was not discussed because elementary education was not in its terms of reference. By the same criterion—length of time at school—the entitlement was prescribed for the peasant boy by the Reverend James Fraser in evidence to the Newcastle Commission (1858–61). 'We must make up our minds to see the last of him as far as school is concerned, at 10 or 11' (quoted in Maclure, 1965, p.75). But W. E. Forster introducing the Elementary Education Bill in 1870 showed that a majority of working class children had no education at all: 'only two fifths of the children of the working classes between the ages of six and ten years are on the registers of the government schools and only one third of those between the ages of ten and twelve' (ibid., p.99).

By 1943 the legitimating ideas underpinning different kinds and different lengths of education for different classes had changed. The system of parallel organisations of elementary and secondary education was directly reflected in a system comprising schools under state control and schools in a private sector, linked by schools under a kind of dual control. Within the private sector the top sections of the capitalist class maintained and still maintains its claim to educational privilege. For the rest of the population, the pressure of various social forces was in process of producing a structure wherein 'secondary education' was beginning to mean a stage of schooling experienced for at least four years by all children from the age of eleven.

The Norwood Report (DES, 1943) still referred to what are called now grammar schools as secondary schools but advocated, 'that within a framework of secondary education the needs of the three broad groups of children which we discussed earlier should be met within the three broad types of secondary education . . . which we think of as the secondary Grammar, the secondary Technical, the secondary Modern' (quoted in Maclure, 1965, p.203). Social class was not even hinted at as a basis of allocation in the Norwood Report though it was quite plain that the secondary modern schools were to be, and actually became, the schools for children of manual workers.

The Report pretended to be dealing with differences in aptitude only, and in all the factors touched upon as influencing the 'evolution of education', the idea of social class is shunned (ibid., p.201):

> the evolution of education has in fact thrown up certain groups, each of which can and must be treated in a way appropriate to itself. Whether such groupings are distinct on strictly psychological grounds, whether they represent kinds of minds, whether the differences are differences in kind or in degree, these are questions which it is not necessary to pursue . . . the recognition of such groupings in educational practice has been justified both during the period of education and in the after-careers of the pupils.

The secondary grammar school was to cater for pupils who could follow a line of logic, discover causes, respond to language, perceive proofs, induction, relatedness and coherence. Other pupils had aptitudes for the application of science and craftsmanship and could go to secondary technical schools. Last were those who found it difficult to go beyond the concrete, the facts, practical matters and whatever was immediate. According to Sir Cyril Norwood and his committee, these were the concrete facts realised in the immediate practical state of affairs whose causes and history 'it was not necessary to pursue'.

The important points are (i) that this definition of secondary education envisaged the continuation of a system complementary to the existing structure of social classes; (ii) that it did so in a way that kept hidden capitalist class purposes. Those who had to be deceived were the sections of the working class who suffered the severest exploitation but who were at the same time the most highly organised: the manual workers. Professional workers might have accepted a definition more frank. But the deceit was believed in by all social classes and occupational groups. There had to be selection. The selection was boasted to be fair, democratic and scientific, carried out in such a way as to set on one side the influence of social class.

Before Norwood, the Spens Report (DES, 1938) had isolated a criterion, seen to be socially neutral in that it was understood to be biologically determined and genetically endowed, for awarding educational advantage. The criterion was the measured amount of the 'General' factor of intelligence as expressed in an Intelligence Quotient (pp.123–5):

> Intellectual development during childhood appears to progress as if it were governed by a single factor usually known as 'general intelligence'. . . . It appears to enter into everything which the child attempts to think, to say or do. . . . Our psychological witnesses assured us that it can be measured approximately by means of intelligence tests.

The distribution of intelligence

Now if intelligence is neutral and if truly 'culture-free' tests have been devised to measure it, the proof that social classes are peopled by truly different kinds of human being, requiring different kinds and durations of education can be established. If the distribution of higher and lower intelligences tallies with social class, correspondingly different educational experience is justified. In Tables 3 and 4 on the class distribution of intelligence there is made out this 'proof'. And by the classification used—a variation on the Registrar General's index—we obtain, incidentally and in addition, a formula suggesting that, given a degree of social mobility, intelligence is a significant determinant of social class.

But the categories in both Tables 3 and 4 are, besides being items in

TABLE 3 *Intelligence of parents and children classified according to occupation**

Class	Occupational category	Children	Adults
I	Higher professional and administrative	120·3	153·2
II	Lower professional, technical, executive	114·6	132·4
III	Highly skilled clerical	109·7	117·1
IV	Skilled	104·5	108·6
V	Semi-skilled	98·2	97·5
VI	Unskilled	92·0	86·8
VII	Casual	89·1	81·6
VIII	Institutional	67·2	57·3

*Source: cited by B. Simon, *Intelligence, Psychology and Education* (1971), p.79.

TABLE 4 *Class distribution of intelligence**

Class	description	mean score	% of sample	No. scoring 50+	% of those in that class	No. scoring —20	% of those in that class
I	Professionals and large employers	51·8	3·7	141	63·8	2	1·4
II	Small employers	42·7	5·3	125	37·4	29	8·7
III	Salaried employees	47·2	3·9	119	50·5	9	0·4
IV	Non-manual wage-earners	43·6	9·1	202	36·2	26	4·7
V	Skilled wage earners	37·2	39·3	549	23·8	368	15·3
VI	Semi-skilled wage earners	33·2	19·8	184	15·3	252	21·0
VII	Unskilled wage earners	31·2	18·9	134	11·7	296	25·9

*Source: *Social Implications of 1947*, Table XXIII, p.7 and Table XXXVIII, p.113, Scottish Mental Survey, London, 1953. Cited by P. W. Musgrave in *Sociology of Education* (1965).

a classification of occupations—graduations of intellectual stimulus. This is borne out especially in the ratings shown in Class II in Table 4. This category, 'Small employers', does not imply, as does every other, a measure of sustained intellectual effort and an appropriate educational experience. Indeed, in that sense it is the odd one out. Because it is the only truly class-relational category, we have a decided 'kink' in the curve.

For those who hold that knowledge, ideas, values, norms, habits and attitudes are learned in a process of socialisation, it will appear from the tables that 'intelligence' is something else that is learned. It is learned better beyond the school for the first four occupations as the higher adult scores in Table 3 indicate. It is learned better at school than at work for the next three occupations. The decisive element appears to be the nature of the occupation. Work, so far as intellectual stimulation is concerned, can be a socialising agency acting in a positive or a negative direction. What is not shown in the Table is the indirect influence of work, through the parent, on the child.

Professor Vernon points out, 'a privileged minority continue to receive intellectual stimulation to 17, 18, 21 or later and are more likely to enter jobs where they use their minds and to indulge in cultural leisure pursuits' (quoted in Williams, 1961, p.167). Raymond Williams writes: 'To take intelligence as a fixed quantity, from the ordinary thinking of mechanical materialism, is a denial of the realities of growth and of intelligence itself in the interest of a particular model of the social system' (ibid.).

The major reasons, then, for the distribution of intelligence as shown in Tables 3 and 4 are: (i) the nature of the occupational structure in capitalist society; (ii) the nature of educational provision in capitalist society. What the tables demonstrate therefore is the extent and mode of intellectual deprivation of the working class.

But the turn had to come from educational policies based on the view expressed by the Barlow Report (DES, 1946) that, 'We need to form an estimate of the proportion of the population inherently fitted to benefit from a University education' (quoted in Maclure, 1965, p.231). The rejection of this policy was carried not only in the Robbins Report but in the major educational reports preceding it: 'The report (Robbins) followed the *Early Leaving* Report, Crowther and Newsome in the recognition of social rather than genetic limitations in the present flow of students' (ibid., p.289).

Four major influences have combined to undermine a virtual monopoly of higher education by the capitalist class. The requirement by employers for more and more technologists, technicians, white-collar workers of all kinds, as well as greater adaptability on the part of manual workers has been a compelling factor in the extension and improvement of education for the working class. Capitalism is an industrial society whose technology demands a suitably educated labour force. But the working class strives for its own interests against those of the capitalists even to the extent of visualising a system without capitalists. It thus creates parties, trade unions and co-operatives, which institutions not only try to educate its own members but also make demands upon society and governments to organise education in ways seen to be beneficial to working-class children. In particular, the Trades Union Congress has long promoted the policy of 'Secondary Education for All'—a policy which found expression in the drive for comprehensive schools by Labour governments after the Second World War.

A third influence is that of the teachers themselves. The National Union of Teachers, representing a force of opinion of men and women engaged in teaching children of the working class, became a major supporting element of efforts to end privilege in education. Asher Tropp writes (1957, p.235):

the elusive concept of 'secondary education for all'. . . was present implicitly in the NUT's educational policy at the turn of the century. . . . During the thirties the NUT concerned itself increasingly with the reconstruction of education and educational research. It had demanded as early as 1928 'that the education of all children over the age of eleven plus in the state aided schools should be administered under a common Code of Regulations, that parity in staffing, equipment and provision of amenities should be secured between present and future types of secondary schools and that secondary education should be free, with adequate maintenance allowances to pupils who are in need of them'.

The fourth influence is the development and direction of educational theory. From training teachers by apprenticeship, through an evolution of teachers' training colleges where some pedagogical theory and a history of educational administration were studied, there have arisen the colleges of education. In these, corresponding to the demand from the working-class movement for well-equipped teachers, a four-sided study of education is entered into: philosophy, history, sociology and psychology. The outcome is a growing awareness in the literature of the importance of social class objectives. There can be little doubt that with the recent steps to make teaching a graduate profession, this trend will continue.

Educational institutions in Britain today embody the outcome of the complex ramifications of class struggle for over a century. The extent and force of the pressures of the working class, of the teachers and of others have yielded a climate in which even those who may wish to do so, will forbear to deny 'that all members of society have a natural right to be educated and that any good society depends on governments accepting this as a duty' (Williams, 1961, p.165). This is the view in the 1944 Education Act which instructed the Minister of Education 'to promote the education of the people of England and Wales and the progressive development of institutions devoted to the purpose and to secure the effective execution . . . of national policy for providing a varied and comprehensive educational service in every area' (Part I, section I).

However, as Raymond Williams points out (1961, pp.165–6),

In practice the system is still deeply affected by other principles . . . one of which is that education in the preparatory and public schools . . . shows the kind of education and the necessary level of investment in it which a particular group accepts as adequate for itself.

From a claim made on grounds of innate superiority as a class there is now operant a naked 'cash justification', the right common to all parents, if they wish, to buy special education. On average the cost in fees per year for a boy boarding at a public school was £510 in 1957; at Eton it was £684 in 1969, at Westminster £672. There are also additional costs for books, stationery, sports gear, clothes and pocket money. Only 2·9 per cent of the children of secondary school age go to these schools, but the allocation of resources indicates the scale of inequality between the tiny dominant capitalist class and the rest (Rubinstein and Stoneman, 1972, p.85).

Whereas the London County Council aimed after the Second World War to provide schools of three-and-a-half acres for up to 1,000 pupils in Inner London (and did not always achieve this ratio) many public schools have an acre or more for each child. Stowe school has 600 boys and 750 acres. In 1967 about 100 independent schools had a teacher-pupil ratio more

generous than 1: 7·5. In 1970 the ratio in primary independent
schools recognised by the DES as efficient was 1: 13·1, in
independent secondary schools as 1: 11·0. This compares with
the 1970 figures for council schools—1: 27·4 in primary schools,
1: 19·1 in secondary moderns, 1: 17·4 in comprehensives and
1: 16·4 in grammar schools.

In *Education: A Framework for Expansion* the Secretary of State
for Education and Science informs us that the national teacher: pupil
ratio had improved, over all, from 1: 25·3 to 1: 22·6. In 1973 of all
primary classes there were still 2·5 per cent with more than forty
registered pupils. We may be sure that these pupils were not in the
preparatory schools.

The kind of education aimed at in the public schools is indicated
by T. B. Bottomore in *Elites and Society* (1964, p.30):

the pattern of events does conform broadly with Marx's scheme;
in England the Reform Act of 1832 gave political power to the
bourgeoisie . . . and the development of public schools created
new opportunities for children from the newly created rich and
industrial and commercial families to be trained for elite
positions.

G. Baron, in *Society, Schools and Progress in England* remarks
(1966, pp.139–40):

The boarding and public schools and the preparatory schools
that feed them form a highly distinctive feature of the
educational and social landscape of England. The implications
of their existence are considerable. They include the acceptance
of the most influential groups being carried on within exclusive
institutions, expressing attitudes subtly different from those
characteristic of the mass of the population. They include also
the acceptance of the assumption—since otherwise they cease
to attract support—that boys who have passed through them
are especially fitted for positions of leadership in all the major
institutions of national life.

'Positions of leadership' is an euphemism convenient to the
necessity of perpetuating the illusion of a grand democratic design
(with some imperfections) governing capitalist society. That the
public schools aim to prepare their pupils for expected positions of
dominance in the economic, political and legal power structure of
capitalist society is shown in the Table 5 from *The Public Schools* by
H. Glennerster and J. Pryke.

TABLE 5 *Percentage of posts filled by those with a public school education*

Conservative Cabinet	(1964)	87
Judges	(1956)	76
Conservative MPs	(1964)	76
Ambassadors	(1953)	70
Lieutenant Generals and above	(1953)	70
Governors of Bank of England	(1958)	67
Bishops	(1953)	66
Chief executives in 100 largest firms	(1963)	64
Air Marshals	(1953)	60
Civil servants above Assistant Secretary	(1950)	59
Directors of leading firms	(1950)	58
Chairman of Government Committees of Enquiry	(1944–60)	35
Members of Royal Commissions	(1960)	51
All City directors	(1958)	47
BBC Governors	(1949–59)	44
Member of Arts and British Councils	(1950–59)	41
Labour Cabinet	(1964)	35
Top managers of 65 largest firms	(1953)	33
Members of Government Research Councils	(1950–5)	31
Labour MPs	(1964)	15

Wakeford in *The Cloistered Elite* (1969, p.228) shows that of the respondents to his questionnaire 33 per cent of past pupils of the public school he researched were employers and managers in central and local government, industry, commerce, etc.—large establishments—whereas 3 to 6 per cent of all economically active males had such status. Of the same sample, self-employed professional workers came to 11 per cent as compared with 0·8 per cent of the population at large, while the comparative figures for professional employees were 25 per cent to 3 per cent.

Technology, social class and education

The essential purpose of the discussion so far has been to bring from obscurity (in most work on the sociology of education) into the forefront the manifestation in educational institutions of the historic antagonism between the proletariat and the bourgeoisie. We should now look at how that antagonism is shaped by the forces of production.

Marxism holds that class structures depend upon the techniques of production and the corresponding division of labour. And it was for this reason that he dealt so closely in *Capital*, volume 1, with their history. The first form of capitalist industry involved 'the decomposition of a process of production into its various successive steps . . . the handicraft continues to be the basis. . . . This narrow technical basis excludes a scientific analysis of any definite process . . . each workman becomes exclusively assigned to a partial function' (1926 edn, Vol. 1, pp.371–2). One outcome is that, 'The one-sidedness and the deficiencies of the detail labourer become perfections when he is part of the collective labourer' (p.397). A second result is that 'Ignorance is the mother of industry as well as of superstition. Reflection and fancy are subject to err; but a habit of moving the hand or foot is independent of either. Manufacturers accordingly prosper where the mind is least consulted.' And a third consequence is that, 'The knowledge, the judgment and the will, which were the craftsmen's before this division of labour was organised in factories, is lost by the detail labourer, is concentrated in the capital that employs them.'

In this mode of production the separation of mental from physical labour is well advanced. More importantly, the wholeness of the capitalist as a human being registers the combination of the fractional individual workmen: 'the labourer is brought face to face with the intellectual potencies of the material process of production as the property of another, and as a ruling power.' In such a relationship of production, education could not be regarded as an economic investment, but as something necessary to offset an undesirable state of affairs such as that outlined by Adam Smith (1970 edn, book V, article II):

> In the progress of the division of labour the employment of the far greater part of those who live by labour, that is, of the great body of people, comes to be confined to a few very simple operations, frequently one or two. But the understandings of the greater part of the men are necessarily formed by their ordinary employments. The man whose life is spent performing a few simple operations . . . has no occasion to exert his understanding. . . . Of the great and extensive interests of his country he is incapable of judging; and . . . he is equally

incapable of defending his country in war . . . that is the state into which the labouring poor . . . must necessarily fall, unless the government take some pains to prevent it. . . . For a very small expense the public can facilitate, can encourage and even impose upon a whole body of people the necessity of acquiring those most essential parts of education.

Marx notes that G. Garnier (Smith's French translator) is disposed to let nature take its course (1926 edn, vol. 1, p.398):

Like all other divisions of labour, that between hand labour and head labour is more pronounced as society becomes richer. This division of labour like every other is an effect of past and a cause of future progress. . . . Ought the government then to work in opposition to this division of labour and to hinder its natural course?

It seems that capitalism agreed with Garnier until another basis for the division of labour, itself immanent in manufacture, took its place.

'In manufacture' says Marx (p.405), 'the revolution in the mode of production begins with labour power, in modern industry it begins with instruments of labour. . . . From the moment that the tool proper is taken from man and fitted into a mechanism, a machine takes the place of a mere implement.' And the machine supersedes the craftsman also in that it 'can bring several tools into play simultaneously' (p.408).

To this change is added eventually the machine's own motive force which in turn can drive more than one machine (p.412).

As soon as tools had been converted from being natural implements of man into implements of a mechanical apparatus, of a machine, the motive mechanism also acquired an independent form, entirely emancipated from the restraints of human strength . . . the motive mechanism grows with the number of machines that are turned simultaneously, and the transmitting mechanism becomes a widespreading apparatus.

Finally (p.414),

A real machine system however, does not take the place of those individual machines until the subject of labour goes through a connected series of detail processes that are carried out by a chain of machines of various kinds, the one supplementing the other.

This mode of production gives rise to a division of labour somewhat different from that which pertained in the manufacturing system (pp.459–60).

Hence in place of the hierarchy of specialised workmen that characterise manufacture, there steps, in the automatic factory a tendency to equalise and reduce to one and the same level every kind of work that has to be done by the minders of the machines. [The division of labour in the factory] is a distribution of workmen among the specialised machines. . . . The essential division is into workmen who are actually employed on the machines (among whom are included a few who look after the engine) and into mere attendants of these workmen. . . . In addition to these two principal classes there is a numerically unimportant class of persons whose occupation it is to look after the whole of the machinery and repair it from time to time. This is a superior class of workmen, some of them scientifically educated, others brought up to a trade: it is distinct from the factory operative class and merely aggregated to it. This division of labour is purely technical.

For the convenience of a greater exploitation of labour, 'the life-long speciality of serving one and the same tool now becomes the life-long speciality of serving one and the same machine' (p.461). As a result, 'The lightening of labour, even, becomes a sort of torture, since the machine does free the labourer from work but deprives the work of all interest' (p.462). And the social relationship typical of all forms of capitalist production (ibid.),

that it is not the workman that employs the instruments of labour but the instruments of labour that employ the labourer . . . for the first time acquires technical and palpable reality. . . . The separation of the intellectual powers of production from manual labour and the conversion of these powers into the might of capital over labour, is . . . finally completed by modern industry erected on the foundation of machinery. The special skill of each individual factory operative vanishes as an infinitesimal quantity before the science, the gigantic physical forces and the mass of labour that are embodied in the factory mechanism and together with that mechanism constitute the power of the master.

The immense leap in productivity brought about by the new techniques gives rise to new occupations. Some of these are necessary as in civil engineering, to build docks, railways, canals and so on.

Others are unnecessary as in the expansion of a servant class during Marx's time.

What is more important however, is that, 'modern industry rent the veil that concealed from men their own processes of production (p.532). In place of the mysteries there is the application of science, the rule of technology (ibid.).

Modern industry never looks upon and treats the existing form of production as final. . . . By means of machines, chemical processes and other methods, it is continually causing changes not only in the technical basis of production but also in the function of the labour process. At the same time it thereby also revolutionises the division of labour in society.

There is a positive side, says Marx, offsetting the terrible conditions imposed by the capitalists using the exploitative opportunities opened up by the factory system (p.534).

Modern industry on the other hand, through its catastrophes, imposes the necessity of recognising as a fundamental law of production, variation of work, consequently fitness of the labourer for varied work, consequently the greatest possible development of his varied aptitudes. . . . Modern industry indeed compels society to replace the detail worker of today . . . by the fully developed individual fit for a variety of labour, ready to face any change of production and to whom the different social functions are but so many modes of giving free scope to his own natural and acquired powers.

It is this underlying fundamental process of changes in the forces of production that needs education and its extension for their guarantee (ibid.).

One step already spontaneously taken towards effecting this revolution is the establishment of technical and agricultural schools, and of 'écoles d'enseignement professionel', in which the children of the working men receive some little instruction in technology and in the practical handling of the various implements of labour. Though the Factory Act, that first and meagre concession wrung from capital, is limited to combining elementary education with work in the factory, there can be no doubt that when the working class comes into power, as inevitably it must, technical instruction, both theoretical and practical, will take its proper place in the working class schools.
The major barrier standing against the fullest incremental progress

from this elemental impulse is capitalism itself. Those relations of production wherein the capitalist class retains its ownership of the means of production and the power to perpetuate them, sustain class-oriented education and transform education's inherent potentiality to end a hierarchic division of labour into its opposite (ibid.).

> There is also no doubt that such revolutionary ferments, the final result of which is the abolition of the old division of labour, are diametrically opposed to the capitalistic form of production, and to the economic status of the labourer corresponding to that form.

But one of the most important characteristics of British capitalism when it had already lost its industrial supremacy even before the First World War was the size of its empire. The finance capitalists and their political representatives saw their interests to lie, not so much in the development of British industry as in the preservation of its exclusive position in trade and financial operations in the colonies and in the dominions. At the close of the first decade of the twentieth century 'close on 2/5 of British imports were no longer paid for by goods; this proportion had risen still higher by the eve of the Second World War' (Dutt, 1953, p.82).

It was only when a net deficit in the balance of payments began to occur during the 1930s that industry's attitude towards science changed. Accordingly, Cotgrove (1958, p.90) is able to report an 'increasing expenditure on research in the 1930s attributable in part to the economic depression'.

The reduction of British capital assets abroad during the Second World War quickened the process. A further acceleration to the demand for scientific manpower has been the new technological revolution since then. The requirements of a modern labour force have altered so much since Marx's time and especially since the First World War that his analysis must be taken forward. Manuel Azcarete (1973) sketches the outlines of a new phase in productive relationships.

> Science is going to become, not just a direct force of production, but a decisive factor in the development of the forces of production, the central productive force of mankind. Production will ever increasingly become the application of science. . . .
> The process of knowledge, of invention, acquires a much more collective character . . . the information potential is becoming decisive, more so than energy potential. . . . The relation of

man to production is being radically transformed. The role of, the need for, man as muscle power, as physical force, as routine (including intellectual routine) is diminishing. What production increasingly demands from man is his creative capacity; that is to say, the maximum development of personality and the abilities of man are becoming a necessity of production, an economic necessity.

Under pressure of these forces, possessors of the most sophisticated labour-power, men and women who have studied into their adulthood and who must continue their studies throughout a lifetime, become increasingly numerous. Their increasing numbers, that is, the more general availability of their accomplishments, places them in the classical position of the proletariat and compels them to recognise as a constant their antagonistic relationship with their employers.

In the third volume of *Capital*, Marx shows how commerce, which complements the productive forces analysed in the first volume, generates other forms of labour in increasing quantity (1926 edn, pp.293–5):

> it is clear that as the scale of production is extended, commercial operations . . . multiply accordingly. . . . This necessitates the employment of commercial wage workers.
>
> The commercial worker . . . belongs to the better paid class of wage workers. . . . Yet the wage tends to fall, even in relation to average labour, with the advance of the capitalist mode of production. This is due partly to the division of labour in the office. . . . Secondly, because the necessary training, knowledge of commercial practices, languages etc., is more and more rapidly, easily, universally and cheaply reproduced with the progress of science and public education the more the capitalist mode of production directs teaching methods, etc., towards practical purposes. The universality of public education enables capitalists to recruit such labourers from classes that formerly had no access to such trades and were accustomed to a lower standard of living. Moreover, this increases supply, and hence competition. With few exceptions, the labour-power of these people is therefore devalued with the progress of capitalist production.

Changes in the forces of production and in the relations of production have not ceased, and they have been reflected, inevitably in the relative proportions of the various sections of the working class. The extent and direction of these changing proportions may be gathered from Table 6.

TABLE 6. *Relative proportions of the total occupied population of Great Britain by major occupation group, 1911–61**

	1911	1921	1931	1951	1961
1 Employers and proprietors	6·7	6·8	6·7	5·0	4·7
2 All white-collar workers	18·7	21·2	23·0	30·9	35·9
(a) Managers and administrators	3·4	3·6	3·7	5·5	5·4
(b) Higher professional	1·0	1·0	1·1	1·9	3·0
(c) Lower professional and technical	3·1	3.5	3·5	4·7	6·0
(d) Foremen and inspectors	1·3	1·4	1·5	2·6	2·9
(e) Clerks	4·5	6·5	6·7	10·4	12·7
(f) Salesmen and shop assistants	5·4	5·1	6·5	5·7	5·9
3 All manual workers	74·6	72·0	70·3	64·2	59·3
Total	100	100	100	100	100

*Source: Research Paper for Royal Commission on Trade Unions and Employers' Associations (1965–8)

The distances between the various sections of the working class have tended to reduce. But this is not matched by a similar reduction between the bourgeoisie and the rest. Production itself—still governed by capitalist relationships—requires knowledge, resources and social co-operation. Nevertheless, capitalists count the worth of their employees in salaries and wages as a cost which must be contained and wherever possible cut back. The creativity of a highly educated labour force is thus at one and the same time appropriated as the legal property of employers and confined to limits imposed by a calculated profitability. Sooner or later these restrictions must be overcome.

Nothing makes the exploitation plainer than the puzzle which presented itself to the Swann Committee trying to frame advice on the channelling of scientists, engineers and technologists into employment. The problem was, and remains, how to deploy abler graduates to meet long-term requirements in the most rational way. The solution is seen in the offer of very high salaries. But the Report (Department of Trade and Industry, 1968) has to recognise the dilemma of the paymasters: that the payment of high salaries to scientists would produce salary demands elsewhere. At the same time the committee complains that, 'Short-term economic fluctuations [in employment] . . . create a disproportionate lack of confidence in industry as an employer'.

To summarise. Marxism shows that groups other than employers and proprietors have in common that they constitute a labour force at the disposal of the capitalist class, but of a kind progressively different, in one major respect, from that necessary to production in the manufacturing period or in the more highly mechanised industry of Marx's own time. This difference is the level of education its members must acquire. This is because education, as one factor among other forces of production, increases its relative strength as a determinant of relations of production and of superstructure. As foreseen by Marx this difference tends also to undermine the hier-archical structure of occupational statuses.

Marxism emphasises also that the capitalist class is an exploiting class standing apart from all other groups who engage in the pro-ductive process, or in the circulation of the commodities produced, or in the training or teaching of the wage labourers, whether they have this or that degree of skill, this or that amount of knowledge, whether their special use is peculiar only to the capitalist mode of production or is of a generally socially useful nature. A hierarchy of occupations is recognised, the precise ordering of which depends upon how technology, the science of the techniques of production, alters the forces of production themselves.

Modern production integrates as never before, and increasingly, the various contributions to the output of commodities. The anti-thesis between the working class in its entirety, and the capitalist class, lies in the fact that intellectuals and 'operatives' are paid a price for their labour-power irrespective of the wealth produced by their common efforts. That wealth remains the property of the capitalist class. Gathering weight is the demand that the function of the scientist and of intellectuals in general be that of social co-operation in the production for society of a plenitude of use-values. To realise this demand there is required a consciousness on their part which places them firmly in association with all manual workers.

Such class consciousness must carry with it the will and action to break the power of a now socially valueless capitalist class. Its progressive elimination as a class can then run simultaneously with the introduction of a socialist system of society. By this historic course of action class division will be ended and a truly classless society inaugurated. A hierarchy of occupational statuses will thus be rendered obsolescent and education will be free to develop in the new recruits to society their latent intellectual, aesthetic, moral and physical powers without reference to positions of dominance or subordination in society.

Chapter 6

Family, class and education

From child-study to family-study

'The family' has an important place in the sociology of education because the children in the classroom at infant, primary and secondary level obviously come from and are very much attached to families. But it has assumed a much more important place in the sociology of education since genetic endowment lost its place in advanced educational thinking as the major determinant of ability. The expression of this change can be witnessed in the report *Early Leaving* (DES, 1954): 'The figures show clearly . . . the extent to which a child's home background influences his performance at school', in the Crowther Report (DES, 1959) which 'showed clearly that among families of manual workers it is still the exception for a child to stay on at school after he is legally free to go', in the Newsom Report (DES, 1963a) 'The results of . . . investigations increasingly indicate that the kind of intelligence which is measured by the tests so far applied is largely an acquired characteristic. . . . Particularly significant (among other factors) are the influences of social and physical environment', in the Robbins Report (DES, 1963b) and in the Plowden Report (DES, 1966).

It is worth while quoting from the Robbins Report (Appendix 1, section 2) at some length to see how the family was isolated as a highly significant social factor in the determination of ability.

Many studies of the distribution of measured ability have brought out the correlation between ability and social class, and it might be held that superior innate intelligence was the only reason why a greater proportion of middle class children than of manual working class children reach higher education. But this is not the case. For, when grammar school children are grouped according to their measured intelligence at the age of eleven as well as their final educational attainment, one finds that among children of a given intelligence a much higher proportion of those from middle class homes reach higher education than those from working class homes.

There are of course differences between families in every social class, differences which are of immediate significance especially to the practising teacher. These differences turn upon what we have previously remarked, that any observed mode of behaviour is derived from a number of actual behaviours, each one of which is nearer to or further from the modal behaviour. But there is more than one mode for the families of our society and these different modes correspond to and express the different social classes and occupational groupings. What we shall try to show is that they do this in a way more directly linked with class antagonisms than is usually shown.

An enormous contribution has been made by the kind of understanding shown in the literature concerning family circumstances besetting children and the way they perform at school. David Glass, for example, in his introduction to *The Home and the School* (Douglas, 1967) points out that it was clear from an examination of the factors affecting illness (and illness affects educational attainment) that 'differences in the quality of "maternal care" played an important part in the different incidence of lower respiratory infections between social classes'. He immediately goes on however, not to exhort working-class mothers to do better, but to point out that 'it was equally clear that the influence of maternal care was most powerful when housing conditions were good; in poor housing conditions even the most conscientious mothers could do relatively little' (p.14).

Housing is also taken up as an important physical determinant of educational attainment of working-class children, by Douglas (p.64):

For manual working class children . . . those whose homes are unsatisfactory (classified by whether or not they are over-crowded, by whether the survey children share their beds or sleep alone, and by whether there is running hot water and a kitchen and bathroom that is not shared with another family) make lower scores in the eleven-year tests than in the eight-year tests.

It is not only housing that is regarded as an important part of environment. Other factors, non-physical in character like the level of education of parents, parental attitudes, the degree of privacy that can be engineered even in a crowded home, ability and readiness to discriminate between schools, number of books to be found in the home, stability of the family, size of the family, age placing of children in the family, have all been used in different and in similar combinations to relate family to social class (or rather occupational categories) and the family to the school. Thus Douglas suggests that (p.65):

parents who are unskilled workers, for example, will often be of low educational attainment, take little interest in their children's school-work, have large families, live in grossly overcrowded homes lacking amenities (unless they are fortunate enough to have a council house) and may well send their children to primary schools which are ill-equipped, with large classes and less than first-rate teaching.

The great importance of such work is that by it the enormous disadvantage suffered by children of manual working-class families in the competition for generous educational provision is exposed. The benefit to be derived from its being revealed lies in the policies for education that can follow . . . policies contributing to a reduction of the competition.

The Plowden Report on primary school education is possibly the most thorough-going piece of work of this kind. Here the influence of the family as the first source of children's experience is emphasised. Consequent demotion of the importance of prediction as to a child's performance at school comes in the labelling of such prediction as self-fulfilling prophecy wherein advanced and well-controlled children get the most interesting and demanding tasks, claim more time and advance furthest. The basis is thus laid for recommending positive discrimination in the allocation of resources for education in favour of 'educational priority areas'.

This recommendation arises from a deepening of the analysis of family influence as the first source of children's experience. Plowden goes beyond a consideration of the family as a unit. It shows how the motivations generated for the child in his family are reinforced by other families in the neighbourhood and by the primary schools in

TABLE 7   *Percentage contribution of parental attitudes, home circumstances and state of schools to variation in educational performance*

Between Schools			Infants	Lower Juniors	Top Juniors	All
	1	Parental attitudes	24	20	39	28
	2	Home circumstances	16	25	17	20
Based on	3	State of school	20	22	12	17
average for	4	Unexplained	40	33	32	35
each school of the variables						
			100	100	100	100
Within Schools						
	1	Parental attitudes	16	15	29	20
	2	Home circumstances	9	9	7	9
Deviation of	3	State of school	14	15	22	17
each pupil	4	Unexplained	61	61	42	54
from the school average						
			100	100	100	100

the neighbourhood. The key to this is the outcome of a National Survey, 'to relate what we could learn about home and school to the attainment of the children'. And the results of that survey are summarised in Table 7 (paragraph 90 of the Report).

Parental attitudes are taken to sum up the age at which they want children to leave school, type of secondary school preferred, number of visits to school, displaying interest in the child's experience there, time spent with children and help with school work, parents' literacy. Home circumstances are estimated from physical amenities, occupation and income of father, size of family, length of parents' education and qualification. The state of the schools refers to its size, size of classes, organisation, the quality of the staff as judged by the head, the quality of the teaching as judged by Her Majesty's Inspectors and competent teachers.

The main purpose of comparing the two tables is to arrive at an understanding of the influence of the neighbourhood. If the neighbourhood was not important the tables would be similar. But there is a big difference and the difference emphasises the importance of neighbourhood as a factor operating on the variables' influence on learning. The difference exists, as the Report puts it, because (p.34)

pupils, parents and teachers in the same school and neighbourhood resemble each other more than they resemble pupils, parents and teachers in general, just as apples growing on the same tree resemble each other more than they resemble apples in general. The apples on a tree in a good situation will do better than those on a tree in a poor situation unless the latter receives special attention.

But in the end even in Plowden, it is the family that is centred upon, for example when it deals with parent-teacher co-operation. For the teachers who are concerned to deal with children and their various activities can meet only with particular parents of individual children if they want contact with other primary socialising agents. Here again, just as in Douglas's *The Home and the School*, the social class and occupational group of the father are taken as significant reference points of expectation and attitude on the part of the teacher. But since schools are not in a position to alter immediately social class relationships, Plowden recommends to teachers that they should engage actively in changing parental attitudes towards their children's schooling. To government it recommends that special assistance be given to schools in educational priority areas.

The view taken here is that families can only be understood as institutions complementary to the ongoing economic processes and the political and other institutions arising therefrom. The ways in which this complementarity is affected turn upon the ways in which the roles played in families sustain mainly roles played in industry. Michael Anderson in his introduction to *The Sociology of the Family* writes (1971, p.7):

The Family in [Western] Societies is, in sum, a collectivity which makes multiple and pressing demands on almost every individual, demands which inevitably influence his ability to participate in and meet the role-demands of other collectivities of which he is a member.

It can be agreed that this is so. But which has greater force? Demands from the family on one of its members to accommodate his role at work to that at home or demands in the opposite direction, demands at work for a modification of the role played in the family? The record of history appears to support the view that the latter pressure is the stronger.

Ronald Fletcher (1962) in a review of sociological generalisations on the family and industrialisation describes Le Play's theory of the move from a patriarchal family to an unstable family 'forced upon it by changing external circumstances' (p.46) and Linton's analysis of the impact of modern industrial society with its demand for a high degree of geographical and occupational mobility and the consequent supplanting of the consanguine type of family by the conjugal type. In both, the functions of the family are listed, and their diminution, as these functions are eroded by industrial society.

Talcott Parsons holds that the type of family which has evolved to meet the requirements of industrial society is, despite high divorce rates, a nuclear family of considerable stability. Its characteristics are that it is a residential unit, 'the family home' being very popular in spite of a high level of geographical and occupational mobility, that it is relatively isolated from other kin as a consequence of the importance of non-kinship units, that the relative economic independence from other kin is made possible by the modern occupational system, that it singles out the husband-father as the primary source of income to become 'the instrumental leader', that the wife-mother's role is predominantly expressive with regard to function. Parsons's view is that 'the family has become, on the "macroscopic" levels almost completely functionless' (1956, p.16). Its individual members participate in economic production, in politics, in schools and so on, but 'not in their roles as family members'. The family in modern industrial society has thus arrived at two 'basic and irreducible functions . . . first, the primary socialisation of children . . . ; second, the stabilisation of the adult personalities of the population of the society'.

The criticisms made of Parsons, which give rise to a cry from Sussman and Burchinal (Anderson, 1971, p.115); 'Understanding of the family as a functional social system interrelated with other social systems in society is possible only by rejection of the isolated nuclear family concept', are founded upon researches which show that nuclear families remain linked with families of origin and other kin. Mutual help and support, it is claimed, are derived from each other by members of 'a network . . . [of] extended family relations . . . composed of nuclear units related by blood and affinal ties' (ibid., p.112). The members of the nuclear units in their different roles support each other financially, socially, during crises of various kinds, in job-finding, childminding and setting up home. Against the isolating tendency of geographical mobility there have to be taken into account the facts that the building of houses in rows in industrial towns gave a physical facility to the links between the units of the extended families and that modern transport effectively reduces whatever separation is made necessary by the new locations of work. Willmott and Young's study, *Family and Kinship in East London*, gives support to this point of view.

Nevertheless Parsons's case remains a strong one, especially when modern urban families are set against the erstwhile rural family and if we may believe that the latter was not unlike the 'small farm family in rural Ireland' described by Arensberg and Kimball. In that type of family the division of labour and long years of intimate association in the acts and events of a common life result in a pattern of total reciprocities between its members (Anderson, 1971, pp.19–20):

> But the point of interest here is that it is the bonds that must
> be dealt with for understanding. . . . Here there is an absolute
> coincidence of social and economic factors within a single
> relationship; to separate their social from their economic
> activities is meaningless. They are one in fact, and, as far as
> the peasants are concerned they are one in name. Thus any of
> the words designating status in the relationship, such as father,
> son, owner, employee, heir, etc., might well be used, but in
> actual practice the first two of them are sufficient to cover all the
> activities of the relationship.

The non-kinship organisations of modern industrial society make this kind of inclusiveness impossible. The connections between such organisations and families are the men, women and children who belong to both kinds of unit: non-kinship organisation and family. But whereas the purposes at work in any of the former will not change readily to meet the needs of any one family, the ties of the extended family are more easily expendable in face of the demands of the non-kinship organisations.

The dominance over kinship networks in urban society by non-kinship structures is strengthened over time by the family cycle. The stages of the cycle may be defined as (i) home-building, a process begun when the marriage 'contract' is final; (ii) child rearing, which continues with parents' diminishing involvement and children's diminishing dependence until children assert their autonomy; (iii) dispersal of children by marriage and/or by departure from the parental home; (iv) final stage, from completion of the dispersal until the death of the spouses. It is shown by B. N. Adams (Anderson, 1971) that frequency of contact, feelings of affection and sense of obligation are greater towards parents than towards siblings or than towards cousins. The solidarity motivation between siblings' families appears to obtain its force from the obligation commonly felt towards parents. Once that sense of obligation ceases on death of parents, or is superseded by a greater sense of duty towards the newly started nuclear families, ties between siblings are further reduced and weakened. It is during the dispersal stage that non-kinship organisations impress most strongly upon its actors the primacy of its claims. During this time, choice of a career, decisions concerning the children's occupational future are of exceptional importance. Increasingly, the changing occupational structure offers a wider variety of options, demands higher levels of education, reduces the importance of assistance from kin and enhances the significance of non-kinship socialising agents (teachers) in their determination of that future.

It is the case too that adequate fulfilment of parental role includes expectations that socialising agencies beyond the family will have a high level of priority in parental attitudes. The reciprocal of teachers' expectations, that in the home favourable facilities will be accorded to education, is a reduction in parents' own roles as possible models for their children's emulation. School-given goals compete with home-oriented activities; punctuality, regular attendance at school and homework shoulder out possibilities of share in the home-based division of labour and reduce the scope of parental leadership; children's possible careers are expected to rank high in parents' aspirations for their children; dispersal from the family home, acceptable at a relatively early age on account of work location is expected to be even more acceptable on account of higher educational achievement opportunity; finally intellectual 'distance' between generations, a by-product of more and better education, is expected also to be welcomed by socially adequate parents.

Although social class is generally referred to in the sociology of the family, often it is in order merely to make a contrast between middle-class and working-class 'life-style', or in order to prove a point concerning functions of the family in modern society. Fletcher comments in this connection that for Britain at any rate there has been in the past, no such thing as the family (1962, p.37):

It is completely impossible to speak about the family in

Britain 'before' or 'after' the industrial revolution in any clear
and definite sense; . . . in the period preceding the more rapid
transformation of Britain to a predominantly industrialized and
urbanized community it would have been impossible to specify
a 'type' of British family which was uniform.

He goes on to discuss kinship units in Britain's history using social
class—not as an incidental feature in their make-up—but as an
economic, political and legal entity determining the nature of
familial interaction and perspective.

To bring us up to date on modern families Fletcher gives an
account of social change without any reference to bitterly contending
interests. The long arduous struggle against powerful opposition to
create and protect trade unions is summarised by a reference to
their 'growing recognition and power'. The sheer physical compul-
sions imposed by a trebling of England's population in less than a
century with its compression into towns, and reforms in education,
in working-class political status, in social services and so on, all are
outcomes of how (ibid., p.117)

Men came increasingly . . . to think it right to take upon
themselves, on the basis of knowledge and reason, the
responsibility for changing society (including the nature and
conditions of the family) in such a way as to achieve a state of
affairs morally and materially better than their experience of
the past.

The result, it is claimed, is that 'the middle classes [and therefore
the Victorian middle-class family] are now no longer in such a
dominant position of expanding wealth and increasing power and
social status' (p.124). Convergently, the working-class family experi-
ences greater prosperity, the opening up of opportunities, social
security, and develops attitudes towards sex and family limitation
largely similar to those of the middle class. 'This leads us to the
conclusion that . . . now, in contemporary Britain, it is possible to
speak of the British Family as a type of family unit which is fairly
uniform throughout society' (p.127).

The objection to Fletcher's view is that he has not carried on into
his analysis of modern family relationships his beginnings of an
insight into those of earlier times. The reason for this failure is his
obvious reluctance to go beyond working conditions that families
encounter to those relationships of production engendering the
working conditions. Had this been attempted Fletcher would have

had to write about capitalism, about family relationships in a capitalist class arising from its exploitative functions and about family relationships in a working class arising from its exploitation. Such an approach would also have saved him from the nonsense that the capitalist class no longer exists.

The family produces labour-power

The logic of capitalism's organisation of production demands, in Weber's terms, 'the most complete possible separation of the enterprise and its conditions of success or failure, from the household or private budgetary unit and its property interests'. A reflection of this separation is the tendency to study family structures and the work situation as almost mutually exclusive spheres. In Marxist terms, the basic motivation of the industrial capitalist in respect of his employees is the lengthening of that portion of the working day during which is created surplus value: or, conversely, the shortening of the portion of the day taken to create the values equal to the market value (wage) of the labour-power expended by the labourer for the whole working day. The market value of that labour-power, however, is determined in exactly the same way as the value of any other commodity; the measure of labour socially necessary to recreate it.

Now all commodities as commodities are exchange values, which is to say that they are only commodities whilst they are in the process of being bought and sold. In production, that which is to become a commodity is an object undergoing the application of chemical, electronic, mechanical, and/or manual operations and is therefore a something of technical interest. Having been bought, in the possession of its consumer, it is a use-value, i.e. valued for the purpose it serves its owner. In the case of commodities which will be used as consumer goods therefore, creation occurs, under strict supervision, at the place of work; but upon being bought, its transformation into an article of use is its new owner's own business. Commodities which are to be used as means of production (raw materials, machine tools) are moved from one level of production to another, to be consumed themselves in creating consumer goods.

Labour-power, however, begins its history outside the factory or office or other work-place. Its production is a complicated process requiring birth, growth, care and socialisation. Thereafter, other processes of recreation are necessary for its availability as a commodity (abstract labour) available on the market and then as a use-value having specific characteristics (concrete labour) only realisable at the place of work. Whereas labour-power is generated, therefore, away from the work-location, its use goes on, under more or less strict supervision at the work-location.

Rapoport and Rapoport in their study 'Family roles and work roles' remark that (1971, p.289):

during the early marriage phase, family-building tasks must
proceed in the context of some effort to establish or maintain
an economic base for the family. For a majority, this means the
husband's job, though it may also involve the wife. Relatively
few couples have no need to work at all.

From the employers' point of view, however, the reverse is the situation: only those who can create and recreate efficiently the labour-power capable of generating a good enough rate of surplus value production, will find a market for their abilities. To mix the Weberian and Marxian orientations: in a capitalist society it is not the job which serves the purpose of building an adequate home, but the home which serves the purpose of providing adequately capable labourers.

Wages, payment for labour-power, have to ensure, as in the price paid for any other commodity in continuous demand, that its quantity and quality will be in sufficient supply. As Marx says in *Capital* (1926 edn, vol. I, pp.190–1):

The owner of labour-power is mortal. If then his appearance in
the market is to be continuous . . . the seller of labour-power
must perpetuate himself, in the way that every living individual
perpetuates himself, by procreation: the labour-power withdrawn
from the market by wear and tear and death must be
continually replaced. . . . Hence the sum of the means of
subsistence received for the production of labour-power must
include the means necessary for the labourer's substitutes,
i.e. his children, in order that this race of peculiar commodity
owners may perpetuate its appearance in the market.

In order to modify the human organism so that it may acquire
skill and handiness in a given branch of industry . . . a special
education or training is requisite and this, on its part costs an
equivalent in commodities of a greater or less amount. This
amount varies according to the more or less complicated
character of the labour-power. The expenses of this education

(excessively small in the case of ordinary labour-power) enter, *pro tanto*, in the total value spent in its production.

Given a capitalist system the working-class family is an institution for ensuring to the market a constant supply of labour-power. Besides the direct exploitation in employment of its individual members there takes place indirectly the exploitation of the family as a whole. During the nineteenth century the factory system at first brought the entire family, previously a home-based working unit, through its gates. Marx hoped that from the resultant dissolution of parental authority a new kind of family would arise: 'modern industry, in over-turning the economical foundations on which was based the traditional family, and the family labour corresponding to it had also unloosened all traditional family ties. The rights of children had to be proclaimed' (p.535). The proclamation was made by the children's Employment Commission in 1866 that exploitation of children's labour is (ibid., pp.535–6),

maintained only because parents are able, without check or hindrance to exercise this arbitrary and mischievous power over their young and tender offspring. . . . Parents must not possess the absolute power of making their children mere 'machines to earn so much weekly wage'. . . . The children and young persons, therefore, in all such cases may justifiably claim from the legislature, as a natural right, that an exemption should be secured to them from what destroys prematurely their physical strength and lowers them in the scale of intellectual and moral beings.

Marx comments (p.536):

it was not however the misuse of parental authority that created the capitalistic exploitation, whether direct or indirect of children's labour; but . . . the capitalistic mode of exploitation which, by sweeping away the economical basis of parental authority, made its exercise degenerate into a mischievous misuse of power.

He goes on to say (ibid.):

However terrible and disgusting the dissolution, under the capitalist system, of the old family ties may appear, nevertheless, modern industry, by assigning . . . an important part in the process of production, outside the domestic sphere, to women, to young persons, and to children of both sexes, creates a new economical foundation for a higher form of the family and of the relations between the sexes . . . the fact of the collective group being composed of individuals of both sexes and all ages must necessarily, under suitable conditions become a source of humane development; although in its spontaneously developed, brutal, capitalistic form, where the labourer exists for the process of production, and not the process of production for the labourer, that fact is a pestiferous source of corruption and slavery.

To proceed further some elucidation is required of the phrase, in the quotation from Robert and Rhona Rappoport, 'need to work'. The sense in which this phrase is used is unambiguous: that social arrangement whereby provisions, shelter, clothing, a modicum of luxury, recreational facilities become available to an employee in return for a readiness to obey his employer for a stipulated number of hours per day. Another way in which 'the need to work' may be felt is as that combination of drives, impulses and instincts, inherently human, to make things, contrive devices, solve problems, attain goals. The two needs can be complementary because artifacts to be made, problems to be solved, goals to be attained are all socially generated. In capitalist society however, the areas of greatest working endeavour are chosen and defined by capitalists. 'Employment' therefore—the contract between capitalist and proletarian—is a process whereby the time of many men is bought to serve purposes determined upon by the owners of the means of production.

This time that is bought is the crux of the relationship between the working-class family and the relations of production in a capitalist society. Change in the working-class family has been in accordance with struggle between the two major social classes of capitalism over the question of working time. The length of the working day, the duration of a working life, the number of hours available from the entire family to a capitalist's purposes, have been decisive in structuring the family, its internal division of labour and the consequent family role patterns.

The division of a labourer's time is into three: (a) working for his employer; (b) renewing his ability to do so; (c) enjoying himself. Marx writes (1926 edn., vol. I, pp.257–8):

The working day has a maximum limit . . . conditioned by two things. First, by the physical bounds of labour-power. Within the 24 hours of a natural day a man can expend only a definite quantity of his vital force. . . . During part of the day this force must rest, sleep; during another part the man has to satisfy other physical needs, to feed, wash and clothe himself. Besides these purely physical limitations the extension of the working day encounters moral ones. The labourer needs time for satisfying his intellectual and social wants, the extent and number of which are conditioned by the general state of social advancement. The working day fluctuates therefore within physical and social bounds. But both these limiting conditions are of a very elastic nature . . . so we find working days of 8, 10, 12, 14, 16, 18 hours i.e. of the most different lengths.

The duration of the working day at any given time and place is determined by the struggle between the interested classes. 'What is a working day? What is the length of time during which capital may consume the labour-power whose daily value it buys?' asks Marx (ibid., p.290). 'It has been seen that to these questions capital replies: the working day contains the full 24 hours with deductions of the few hours of repose without which labour-power absolutely refuses its services again'.

There stems from the inseparability of the commodity labour-power from the labourer, from its generation and regeneration at home and its consumption at work, from the elasticity of the working day a unique characteristic (ibid., p.259).

The capitalist maintains his right as a purchaser when he tries to make the working day as long as possible. . . . On the other hand . . . the labourer maintains his right as a seller when he wishes to reduce the working day to one of definite normal duration. There is therefore, an antimony, right against right, both equally bearing the seal of the law of exchanges. Between equal rights force decides. Hence it is that in the history of capitalist production, the determination of what is a working day, presents itself as the result of a struggle, a struggle between collective capital, i.e. the class of capitalists and collective labour, i.e. the working class.

The struggle over the working day has not been a matter simply of standardising what hours per day were to be expected from an individual labourer. An important part of that struggle was the identification of members of the working-class family whose subjection to direct exploitation should be delayed or limited. Hence the long and continuing battle for legislation to take children out of the factories and for a progressive rise in the age of prohibition of employment. The same engagement is carried forward in a new way when the demand is made to raise the school-leaving age. Taking the view, therefore, that the family under capitalism is a unit for generating labour-power for sale upon the market, the length of the working day is the number of hours obtained by the capitalist from all the members of the family. The elimination of children from the directly exploitative situation is therefore a curtailment of time available to the capitalist.

Hence too, the sanction for married women to stay at home stems in large part from the convenience seen to inhere in a division of labour corresponding to modern industrial productive relations. This is clearly brought out in Ducpetiaux's calculation, cited by Marx, that an entire working-class family earns less than the cost of feeding one prisoner (ibid., p.739).

In the family taken as typical we have calculated all possible resources. But in ascribing wages to the mother of the family we raise the question of the direction of the household. How will its internal economy be cared for? Who will look after the children? Who will get the meals? do the washing and mending? This is the dilemma incessantly presented to the labourers.

The factory produces household roles

Here is defined the so-called expressive role of the wife-mother arising as one element in the division of labour between husband and wife. Husband in the factory or pit: wife in the home. It is a mistake to see this division of labour as home based. It is factory based unless the economy is directed to satisfy social needs. The wife-mother expressive role must (i) ensure the proper fulfilment of her husband's instrumental role in his performance as a labourer, and, (ii) ensure their children's proper availability for similar roles. The husband for his part demands that his wife fulfil efficiently this function and in so doing defines, at home, his identity as a labourer in the factory. The conditions exist therefore for a transference to the labourer's home of personal-functional relationships echoing the capitalist-labourer relationship: the wife becomes the labourer's labourer.

Engels saw this division of labour, as it is derived from productive relations, to be the last major barrier to the rule of sex love in proletarian marriages. When he explored the ways in which relations of production manifested themselves in family structure, he concerned himself largely with the conditions generating sex war in the bourgeois family: 'monogamous marriage comes on the scene as the subjugation of one sex by another; it announces a struggle between the sexes unknown throughout the whole previous pre-historic period' (1972 edn, p.128). Its original intention was 'to make the man supreme in the family and to propagate, as the future heirs to his wealth, children indisputably his own' (ibid.). The subjection of women was generalised in society by monogamy's first contradiction, —hetaerism (concubinage and prostitution) but also by its second contradiction, adultery, women obtained their revenge. The bourgeois marriage was always subject, in one degree or another, to control by the property relations of its members. Hence the tendency for monogamy, with its contradictions, to persist in bourgeois marriages.

Because of the absence of property and inheritance, the domination of the proletarian husband over his wife and over his children ceased to be in force. 'Sex love in the relationship with a woman becomes and can only become the real rule among the oppressed classes, which means today among the proletariat—whether this relation is sanctioned or not' (p.135). And he saw the possibility of economic independence of the proletarian wife as the guarantee that sex love would be the strongest marriage bond (ibid.):

> And now that large scale industry has taken the wife out of the home onto the labour market and into the factory, and made her often breadwinner of the family, no basis of any kind of male supremacy is left in the proletarian household, except, perhaps for something of the brutality toward women that has spread since the introduction of monogamy . . . if two people cannot get on they prefer to separate. In short, proletarian marriage is monogomous in the etymological sense of the word, but not at all in its historical sense.

Capitalism imposes a barrier to the full realisation of these possibilities for the proletarian wife. And it does so precisely because it insists upon the function of the working-class family as a supplier of labour-power both immediately and prospectively. That is to say, it insists upon retaining the working-class family as an economic productive unit, a unit for the production of labour-power. The road to social production was opened by (p.137)

> large-scale industry . . . only to the proletarian wife. But it was opened in such a manner that, if she carries out her duties in

the private service of her family, she remains excluded from public production and unable to earn; and if she wants to take her part in public production and earn independently, she cannot carry out family duties.

When women are in employment an associated barrier to equal status with men is encountered in unequal rates of pay. This in itself is a force in the direction of making working-class families function in accordance with capitalist purpose. But in general, when wives are at work, the likelihood that instrumental roles become common to the spouses is undoubtedly greater. Similarly the problems of coping with expressive roles are open to solutions on a basis of equity.

The foregoing discussion emphasises the dominating compulsion of work roles in determining relationships in the home. In this way too, the home's part in renewing a worker's ability to produce is also stressed. What is not indicated is the influence of time used, in family life, by its members, for emotional, intellectual, social and aesthetic fulfilment. The 'working day' with its echoes at home crowds out the 'living day'. But the emphasis is correct. There are the facts that 'the job', in varying degrees, itself yields these satisfactions and frustrations, and that it furnishes the wage determining life-style.

This force is at work in the socialisation of children. Attitudes to education and to school work apart, the realities of the social relations governing availability of shelter, of clothing and of sustenance matter far more than their material quality. This greater importance inheres in the children's having to learn precisely these meanings and in the fact that these relationships condition the conditions of their lives. The precedence of the husband-father's external role as a workman makes itself felt in the allocation of time available to his internal role-set as a father and as a husband. The primacy of his role as an earner, whereby the connection between home and work is established by the responses from the wife-mother to this role. Not least, the immense power of 'the job'—governing style of life, associations, morale—over the pair who, to their children, are powerful persons, gives it god-like proportions and qualities.

Not only from inter-adult behaviours does a child draw his awareness of the supreme power of employment. The worries and hopes of parents turn ever and again from problems of physical, mental and social growth of their children to the ultimate marketability of their labour-power. Possible occupations are understood, in accordance with parental suggestion, to be more or less realistic. The life experience of parents, their knowledge of what counts in the future chances of bread-winning comes into play at an early age in making sure that their children will have a good start in the educational competition for selection. Their purpose is to help their children win a good bargaining position in the competitive labour market.

It has been indicated that if the emphasis on the proletarian family as a unit in society for producing labour power as a commodity is justified, it is certainly not the whole story. For one thing, as Marx pointed out, labour has two characteristics, it is, under capitalism, a commodity for sale upon the market with an exchange-value, but is also a use-value. That is, it has a concrete as well as a general aspect. In its concrete aspect labour makes the labourer—not a mere 'seller of labour-power' on the labour market, not a mere 'embodiment of labour-power' in the productive process—but a socially active worker achieving in co-operation with others, personal fulfilment. Work in this sense is creative of human welfare and affords satisfactions not otherwise obtainable.

Again, a definition of the working-class family as being only a unit for producing labour-power as a commodity would render the struggle for a shorter working day meaningless. It is demanded that that part of the day which is not expenditure or recreation of labour-power should be extended at the expense of the former. The shorter the working day and working week, the longer annual and seasonal holidays, the more there is time for emotional, physical, intellectual, social and aesthetic fulfilment. The struggle of the working class thus joins a demand for time in which to live, to one in which the sources of a fuller life—in all its aspects—are made available to its members. Here is the basic motivation that brought the labour movement consistently to pursue the objective of secondary education for all children rather than the competitive philosophy enshrined in the slogan of 'equality of opportunity' in education.

Characteristics of the modern working-class family seen to include therefore:

(1) current and prospective exploitation by capitalism of the family as a unit and of its individual members by (a) a division of labour in the home which facilitates direct exploitation of the male spouse and through him of his wife, (b) direct exploitation of the wife

too during certain phases of the family cycle, (c) socialisation of the children—including education—in the direction of anticipated exploitation;

(2) struggle as a family and through non-kinship organisation, to reduce the scope and intensity of exploitation by (a) readiness to engage in work as one mode of social life, (b) readiness to effect a home-based division of labour in accordance with different phases of the family cycle to effect this and other kinds of personal development of its members, (c) socialisation of children—including education—in the direction of becoming mature, independent, cultured persons;

(3) struggle to insulate the family and its members from the harsher effects of market conditions upon price and conditions of sale of labour-power by demands for a variety of social services;

(4) dependence for maintenance of home and life upon earnings from sale of labour-power (or upon social security benefits) and absence of private property on a scale sufficient to reduce this dependence materially;

(5) consequent appearance of hardship during the second, child-rearing phase of the family cycle and during the fourth phase when reduced earnings occur;

(6) dependence for educational facilities upon arrangements made by state institutions and therefore subject to considerable influence from the capitalist class.

The bourgeois family

A little had already been said about the bourgeois family—that is, families of members of the capitalist class. A most important characteristic of a family in this social class is that it is linked to the economy, not by the application of labour to the productive process but by its influence over the nature and distribution of the product. In this connection, Marx (1926 edn, vol. II, chapter XX), in his analysis of simple reproduction with its Division I where means of production are produced and Division II where articles of consumption are produced, directs attention to the further bifurcation of Division II into (a) production of necessities of life and (b) production of luxuries. In that statement we are shown a demand for products which will enter into the consumption only of capitalists, but which must be a part of the totality of goods created by labour.

Marx indicates here that certain labourers are themselves luxuries.

Earlier, in *Capital* (1926 edn, vol. I, p.488) Marx noted that 'the extraordinary productiveness of modern industry . . . allows of the unproductive employment of a larger and larger part of the working class'. He estimated that of 'eight millions of the two sexes of every age . . . in any way engaged in industry, commerce or finance' in 1861 1,208,648 persons worked as domestic servants.

The contemporary scene has unfolded against a background of family nucleation, technological development, changing types of employment and a vast output of new products. The results are manifest in an enormous growth in the number of households accompanying their reduction in size. 'Separate occupiers rose from just over 5 million in 1871 to just over 7 million in 1901. . . . By 1921 the number of private families had grown to 8¾ million and in 1931 there were just over 10 million. . . . In 1951 there were just over 13 million private householders' (Marsh, 1968, pp.48–52). The figure given for 1961 is 14·6 million. Moreover, in these households a revolution in housekeeping technology has been effected.

Thus the lesser bourgeoisie find it possible to manage with reduced attention from servants. And in any case, enterprise has been able to use productivity to transform the 'servant class' into a 'service industry' including a proliferation of luxury flats, hotels, clubs and other commercialised forms of personal service. The outcome has been a sharp decline in the number of domestic servants, which stood at 103,000 in 1961.

Nevertheless, as an occupational group they are still to be found though the full time resident seems to be giving way to the full time non-resident servant. A random look at *The Times* domestic vacancy column for 29 September 1971 showed that there were required: 6 married couples to perform a range of female duties including cook, housekeeper, and cook's help, and of male duties including those of chauffeur, houseman, handyman, gardener; 15 single females to perform nanny or nanny's help duties; 11 single females to act as housekeeper/cooks; and 5 single males to act as houseman, butler or chauffeur. Table 8 brings together the information available from the vacancy column.

The intention here is not to analyse the terms of domestic service but to show that the division of labour in the capitalist household involves the use of persons not in the family in ways that imply inferior status. The female spouse of such a family carries out her

TABLE 8 *Domestic vacancies*

Number of posts	Personnel required	Accommodation prospect associated with position		
		Live in	Live out	Self-contained rent-free flat or house
6	Couples	2	–	4
15	Nannies, etc.	7	4	4
11	Housekeeper/Cook	5	3	3
5	Single males	1	3	1
37		15	10	12

expressive tasks by arranging for other persons to do the work associated with them. This ensures for the wife-mother a commanding role, in miniature not unlike her husband's in the sphere of production. For satisfaction in socially useful work the bourgeois substitutes a drive to accumulate wealth, elevating this to a criterion of worth. The bourgeois wife is made dependent by marriage but she finds compensation in managing rather than performing the household chores. The promotion of both forms of work-evasion to a high place in the order of values is registered in the low currency attached to work performance. The daughters of the bourgeoisie become acutely aware that any future status will be determined by a future husband's economic success. Dissatisfied with the uncertainty of power whilst they are spinsters, and with its pale reflection if they become wives, they seek entry into the world of work. But it is not work in the factory or the office that they want. Some find direct entry into the business world, but certain professional employment might also do. The sons of capitalists are disposed by self-interest as well as by the terms of their socialisation experience to perpetuate the roles of their fathers.

The socialisation of children of the capitalist family proceeds therefore in a web of interactions and meanings which induce in them expectations consonant with an active role in exploitation. Their direct identity-forming experience includes habituation to master-servant relationships, to a style of living based on great economic advantage, and to echoes of father's capitalist role in industry and commerce.

The bourgeois family complements proletarian families first of all at the point of production—in the factory. Lane and Roberts in *Strike at Pilkington's* (1971) show, concretely, how a capitalist extended network interacts with working-class families.

From what they report it appears that the firm's existence has given to Pilkington's a high degree of integration and of continuity of common purpose as a family (p.36):

Of the two original Pilkington glassmen, William, with his wife's assistance, produced six sons and six daughters while Richard managed four sons. Of these, two sons of each took an active part in the business: these sons produced nine sons and fourteen daughters. From this third generation the firm captured eight of the sons, and three of the daughters made sufficiently good marriages to provide three sons suitable for fourth generation directorships. The four other fourth-generation family directors are descended through the male line. The fourth generation who were board members in 1959 had produced seven sons and thirteen daughters: insufficient sons, when drop-outs are accounted for, to ensure a family majority on the board in the fifth generation.

Thus it is that family places are now augmented by six who have been promoted from managerial positions.

Market manipulation even for the sale of glass requires a sense of vocation: 'There has obviously been a rare degree of dedication of purpose, for the firm could not otherwise have grown to its present size and remained under family control' (p.37). A religious dimension has been given to this economic purpose by the family's strong connections with the church. In all probability this helps considerably in bringing others to share their sense and direction of moral duty. But conviction alone is not relied upon (p.38).

Coupled with this moral dedication to the firm has been a severely paternal attitude towards employees. . . . Pilkingtons have attempted to exact from their employees the same devotion to duty that they have set for themselves. Those who have been faithful have been rewarded—those who have been naughty have been smacked.

If, in spite of exhortation from the pulpit and threat of economic penalties, private property nevertheless suffers offence, there are other control agencies participated in by the Pilkington family. 'Successive generations of Pilkingtons have been JPs on the St.

Helens bench, local councillors and aldermen [as well as] commanding officers of the local Territorial Army Unit' (ibid.).

It has been noted that if the Pilkingtons 'have lived comfortably, they have not lived flamboyantly' (p.37). Their thrift has been displayed also in their wages policies and in welfare arrangements whose motivation was avowedly that of work efficiency. As Lane and Roberts note, this latter meant that 'workers are as a matter of fact units of manpower but they must not be treated as if they are' (p.44). To study the activities of this capitalist extended family and how the various roles of its members link together is to be impressed by its similarity—in miniature—to the larger capitalism's economic and power structure within which it operates.

Proletarian families are attacked by a similar kind of complementarity at their homes. Mortgage interest is one other way of appropriating for capitalist families a portion of the labourer's product. And so is rent—not to mention land-value payments included in the price of a house. An indirect but efficient way of achieving a similar result is the use of local government as agencies for the collection and payment of interest on capital borrowed 'to finance' the building of working-class homes.

It would not be true to claim that every capitalist family functions as directly as Pilkington's in its control over working-class families. But it is certain that directly or indirectly every capitalist family engages in the perpetuation of its economic and social privileges. Its members assume, in the appropriate institutions, financial, industrial, political, legal, military, ideological and religious roles in order to do this. Socialisation at home and at school of the children of such families therefore proceeds accordingly.

Characteristics of the modern capitalist family seem to include therefore:

(1) possession of wealth enough to form a basis for such continuous exploitation of labour-power as will yield sufficient surplus-value to live on;

(2) current and prospective exploitation, of wage and salary earners in productive employment, by the family as a unit and by its individual members;

(3) a division of labour in the household which secures service from persons not related to the family, this service being a mode of surplus value expenditure;

(4) the assignment thereby of secondary exploitative roles to

housewives and to the children of the family;

(5) socialisation of the children—including their education—in the direction of anticipated exploiting roles;

(6) effort as a family, and through non-kinship organisations to maintain and extend economic power, by recruitment of offspring and of other kin to direct the protection and legitimation of that power;

(7) freedom from uncertainties of an economic kind during all phases of the family cycle;

(8) maintenance of family solidarity and loyalty by economic ties and by inheritance;

(9) access to special educational provision for children;

(10) influence by means of membership of non-kinship organisations, over state educational provision for children of the working class.

Chapter 7

Language and deprivation

Gouldner, Stalin and Marxism

Because it raises certain general issues concerning not only Marxism but also language and culture, it will be convenient to refer to Professor Alvin W. Gouldner's remarks in *The Coming Crisis of Western Sociology* (1970, pp.453–4) on Joseph Stalin's placing of language in the Marxist sociological framework.

> Stalin's position, in effect added a third category to the traditional Marxist distinction between infra-structure and super-structure, and this was accepted by Soviet scholars. This third category includes social phenomena, such as language—which in an interesting convergence with Parsons is a prerequisite of social development—as well as mathematics, symbolic logic, and the facts (as opposed to interpretations) of science. These, it seems, are now regarded as independent of the economic infra-structure and do not vary with changes in it.

> It is clear that this issue was not half so important in its specific implications for language as in its general consequences for classical Marxism as a theoretical system. Classical Marxism had dichotomised the world of social phenomena holding that everything in it was either part of the economic infra-structure or part of the super-structure. What Stalin was, in effect, doing was acknowledging that this conceptual dichotomy so central to Marxism was unworkable. The position he took had inevitably to create pressure for a more general and drastic overhauling of Marxism and not merely of its peripheral elements but of its very fundamentals.

The first matter to clear up is the view of Marxism as a theoretical system which 'had dichotomised the world of social phenomena [into] economic infra-structure [and] social super-structure'. It is difficult to see how this can be inferred from the widely known, oft-quoted formula contained in a single paragraph in the Preface to *An Introduction to a Critique of Political Economy*. Marx declares (1918 edn., pp.11–13):

> In the social production which men carry on they enter into definite relations . . . ; these relations of production correspond to a definite stage of development of their material powers of production.

Unless it is argued that social production is not part of the world of social phenomena we must conclude that what is imputed to Marxism by Gouldner is quite mistaken. If we are to make a dichotomy it must be found in Marxism to lie in the contradiction— not between superstructure and relations of production—but between relations of production and forces of production. Thus, in the same paragraph:

> At a certain stage of their development, the material forces of production in society come into conflict with the existing relations of production. . . . [Again], in considering such transformation [social revolutions] the distinction should always be made between the material transformation of the economic conditions of production . . . and the legal [economic relations, property rights, etc.], political, religious, aesthetic or philosophic—in short ideological forms in which men become conscious of this conflict and fight it out.

And again: 'No social order ever disappears before all the productive forces . . . have been developed; and new higher relations of production never appear before the material conditions of their existence have matured.' Yet again: 'The bourgeois relations of production are the last antagonistic form of the social process of production . . . ; at the same time the productive forces developing in the womb of bourgeois society create the material conditions for the solution of that antagonism.'

It is a commonplace that all subsequent Marxist writings have been oriented to a conceptual framework which visualises superstructure's dependence on economic relations, and economic relations' dependence upon, and ultimate antagonism with, forces of production. Stalin's position then, added nothing to Marxism when it referred to social forces other than economic relations and superstructure.

We must now clear whether Stalin regarded language as belonging to a category outside this conceptual framework. A difficulty seems to arise in the employment of the term 'basis' when Stalin says, 'The basis is the economic structure of society', and goes on to declare that, 'Language is not a product of one or another basis' (1950, pp.3–4). This difficulty vanishes as soon as Stalin indicates where, in a Marxist view, language does belong (p.5).

> In this respect, while it differs in principle from the super-structure, language does not differ from the implements of production, from machines, let us say, which are as indifferent to classes as is language and may, like it, equally serve a capitalist system and a socialist system.

It becomes quite clear from this, and as we read on, (i) that basis and economic structure are, in Stalin's mind, quite justifiably, the productive relations discussed by Marx, (ii) that in Stalin's view, language must be linked principally with forces of production. Since mathematics, science, logic and certain classes of facts, also belong to the forces of production category, it becomes clear that Stalin added no new category to this component of Marxist thought. Neither is there any suggestion that this theory is being found to be unworkable, as it would be if language were assigned to super-structure. For the difference between basis together with super-structure on the one hand and forces of production on the other, is the same as the difference between the former and language. 'The super-structure is the product of one epoch. Language on the contrary [like forces of production] is the product of a whole number of epochs in the course of which it takes shape, is enriched, develops and is polished' (ibid., p.6).

Stalin took the Marxist view that language is directly linked with the work of human beings at any stage of their social development (p.16):

> Exchange of ideas is a constant and vital necessity, for without it, it is impossible to co-ordinate the actions of people against the forces of nature, in the struggle to produce the necessary material values; without it, it is impossible to ensure the success of society's productive activity, and, hence the very existence of social production becomes impossible. Consequently without a language . . . society . . . must disintegrate and cease to exist as a society.

What is strange is that in this discussion Stalin makes no reference to what Engels wrote on language in his chapter on 'The Part Played by Labour in the Transition from Ape to Man' (1972 edn.). Engels in this chapter concentrates on the development of the hand as being crucial in this evolution and remarks, 'Thus the hand is not only the organ of labour, it is also the product of labour' (p.252). He notes that at the same time as this development, man's predecessors were gregarious. However (pp.253–4),

the development of labour necessarily helped to bring members of society closer together by increasing the bases of mutual support and joint activity. . . . In short, men in the making arrived at the point where they had something to say to each other. Necessity created the organ; the undeveloped larynx of the ape was slowly but surely transformed by modulation to produce constantly more developed modulation and the organs of the mouth gradually learned to pronounce one articulate sound after another.

This is the kind of thinking which results when explanations for human behaviour are looked for—as Marxists look for them—in labour as the basis of human existence. But to what extent do these ideas of Engels find support almost a century later?

Orr and Campanari (De Cecco, 1966, pp.63–8) hold that the problem of the emergence of language involves on the one hand, a study of the evolution of the physiological and neurological pre-requisites of language which are the organs of hearing and of speech; but on the other hand, because 'there are minimal internal neuro-anatomical pathways between speaking and hearing' connections between them must also be sought beyond the human being as an organism, in his environment. They therefore consider language as a circuit with two domains. External to each person is the 'outside world of sounds and people, or ecology and culture and of environmental stimulus'. Internally is 'the domain of nerve impulses and synapse, dream and symbol and adaptive capacity'. The ears are the receptors for sounds at one nexus of the person with his world, the speech organs are the emitting structure completing and restarting the circuit.

The basic relationship between the two worlds is founded upon the ability and the need of the human being to symbolise. The symbol is a stored image, 'a coded neurological pattern', of the external world. This stored imagery has two allied consequences for man.

Because this symbolism allows internal functional communication between speech and hearing, immediate interaction with significant events in the external world can be discontinuous.

It is deduced from these characteristics of language and its practice and transmission, that the social aspects of language in groups using vocalisations, must have come before the 'genetic mutations which could be advantageously selected'. Orr and Campanari go on to suggest that since language might have conferred survival advantages only with fuller development, it could well have come into being as a by-product of other evolutionary change—changes in manual dexterity and in the corresponding brain structure. 'It is in this fact— the hand with its precise, complex, highly integrated faculties evolved concomitantly with the marked expansion of the cerebral cortex in size and complexity and both of these apparently parallel the development of language—that is so challenging.'

We can see at once that although the main direction of Engels's enquiry is vindicated by modern research, he underestimated the qualitative change in thinking power accompanying the evolution of human beings. For the important element in human speech is the genetically endowed mental ability to make symbols. As Eleanor Burke Leacock remarks in a footnote to Engels's discussion concerning the pressure on vocal organs to accommodate to man's need for communication (Engels, 1972 edn, p.254):

Actual pronounciation is not the main problem; instead it is the intellectual feat of symbolisation basic to language.

The organic independence of the power and apparatus of symbolisation from the receptors and emitting structures has been convincingly discussed by Ernst Cassirer in *An Essay on Man* (1970 edn). He distinguishes between propositional and emotional language and parallels this with the distinction between the sign and the symbol. Signs are operators and are part of an animal's impulse to 'practical imagination and intelligence'. The symbol is a qualitatively different thing. The symbol's flexibility as a means of cognising the world, its universality of application (there's a name for everything) and its enablement of rational thought characterises and makes possible human culture. The ability to make symbols is man's alone. But this use is not dependent on speech or on hearing, as can be seen by reference to the case of Helen Keller, a blind, deaf, mute whose life was transformed when she learned by means of the manual alphabet that everything has a name, and again, though not as dramatically, in the case of Laura Bridgeman.

Approximating to Cassirer's position is that of Vygotsky. Exploring what he calls the genetic roots of thought and language Vygotsky declares, 'In principle language does not depend upon the nature of its material. The medium is beside the point: what matters is the functional use of signs, any signs that could play a role corresponding to that of speech in humans' (1962, p.38). This functional use is possible only by humans because they alone are so constituted genetically as to adapt themselves intellectually to their world. Like Cassirer, by reference to the work of Koehler and Buehler who are interested in comparing the thought processes of anthropoids with those of children, Vygotsky concludes that the vocal behaviour of chimpanzees is closely related to their affective states and to their contact with others of their kind. Their limited intellectual behaviour is understood to rely, not on memory traces, but on the situation as it is seen without the lapse of time. Moreover, this kind of behaviour is not accompanied by speech. 'The close correspondence between thought and speech characteristic of man is absent in anthropoids' (ibid., p.41).

The work of Charlotte Buehler is closely remarked upon by Vygotsky. Buehler showed that the child's actions at the tenth, eleventh and twelfth months were so exactly like those of chimpanzees that the phase could be called the chimpanzoid stage. But, because, without language corresponding to it, the child displays inventiveness at this age, because before the advent of intellectual speech there is device (and therefore thought) relating mechanical means to ends, the conclusion is reached by Vygotsky that thought and speech have independent starting points in the lives of children. Language may be social and emotional from the outset but it becomes linked with thought only later: 'at a certain moment [at about two years] the curves of thought and speech meet and initiate a new form of behaviour' (ibid., p.43).

The fact that vocalisation expresses, in the first place, the social-emotional responses on the part of a child does not mean for Vygotsky that the societal work of language is restricted to this. Vygotsky adopts word-meaning, a unit of verbal thought, as his basic tool for investigating language and thought. He explains very carefully that he does so because word-meaning 'retains all the basic properties of the whole, which cannot be further divided without losing them' (p.4). These properties refer to the work of word-meaning (i) as a unit of intellectual construction, and (ii) as an element facilitating human communication and social intercourse. Individual experience can only become communicable when it is organised in categories ultimately validated by the participants in society through convention and custom. Meanings are units of these tacitly shared agreements. True, the generalisations implicit in categories (and therefore in meanings) greatly simplify the world of experience. But without this generalisation experience could not be transformed into symbols. And without the symbols higher forms of human intercourse would not be possible. In short, society has to have a mediating system for the exchange of what is rational and intentional amongst its members. That mediating system is language whose basic unit is a unit of word-meaning.

The foregoing discussion on the emergence of language in the course of the evolution of human life and labour should have one element added if it is to comply with a Marxist orientation. This is that the symbol represents a representation in man of external reality of a social or natural order. When the utterance, 'The boat is sunk', is made, not symbols, not word order, nor the sounds engage the attention of the crew but the image of the reality and the imaginings of its consequences. The meaning taken from the symbols is the meaning represented by the symbols. On this view the human power to symbolise a fact or a possibility, a deed or an intention, serves the human power to know a fact or a deed, to conceive a possibility or an intention.

From what has gone before, it appears that Joseph Stalin's notion of language as belonging to the category of 'forces of production' may be added to. It may be said that language is, besides, a naturally evolved human attribute as much as are the human hand, the human brain, the capacity to produce surplus-value.

Relativism or universalism?

Edward Sapir also emphasised the universality of language 'Language is an essentially perfect means of expression and communication among every known people' as well as its taking the form everywhere of 'a system of phonetic symbols of thought and feeling' (1926, p.1). Sapir's way of drawing attention to the impulse to symbolise as the key to understanding language was by reference to the tongue. The tongue is a major organ of speech. Yet, speech constitutes for it only a secondary network of physiological activities, bearing no correspondence to its primary functions. It is as if the impulse to symbolise had suborned tongue and lips and vocal chords for its complicated work.

But symbolism requires a complex of referents—or rather, it is the complex of referents, the culture, which is what has to be symbolised (ibid., p.6).

Language is felt to be a perfect symbolic system . . . for the handling of all references and meanings that a given culture is capable of, whether these be in the form of actual communications or in that of such ideal substitutes of communication as thinking.

It is important to understand here that Sapir, like Vygotsky, does not endorse the notion that communication is the be-all and end-all of language (p.15).

The primary function of language is generally said to be communication. There can be no quarrel with this so long as it is distinctly understood that there may be communication without overt speech and that language is highly relevant to situations which are not obviously of a communicative sort. . . . It is best to admit that language is primarily a vocal actualisation of the tendency to see realities symbolically.

The interplay between language and culture is no simple matter in Sapir's view. It is true that culture change influences language, but only as a 'further application of principles already in use', and this is exemplified in the relative slowness of linguistic as compared with culture change. Arising from the greater stability of language is its tendency for its structure to 'predetermine for us certain modes of observation and interpretation'. As a consequence language is simultaneously a help and a hindrance to the exploration of experience, the specific modes of which manifest themselves 'in the subtler meanings of different cultures'.

The union of language with culture makes it inevitable that certain problems associated with our understanding of cultures should attach also to our understanding of language. One of these problems is whether or not cultures may be compared one with another in like terms, whether their institutions may be thus compared, and whether they may be placed somewhere on a developmental scale or judged against each other by criteria of progress. Relativism, a strong trend in opposition to this kind of comparability, to commensurability, is current among anthropologists and extends to language. The position is described by Floyd G. Lounsbury in an article 'Language and culture' (1970, p.8):

A cryptanalyst at least can assume that, when a cipher is cracked, the hidden message will become understandable and translatable. Anthropologists have been rather less sure about this in their ethnographic analogue. To the contrary, the more extreme cultural relativists among them have become quite convinced of the nonequivalence and untranslatability of concepts from different social and cultural systems. . . and the relativity of culture has its analogue, or correlate, in a relativity of the meaning content of language.

Sapir stated his own relativist position as follows (cited by Lounsbury, 1970, p.9):

Inasmuch as languages differ very widely in their systematisation of fundamental concepts, they tend to be only loosely equivalent to each other as symbolic devices and are, as a matter of fact, incommensurable in the sense in which two systems of points in a plane are, on the whole, incommensurable to each other if they are plotted out with reference to different systems of co-ordinates.

As Lounsbury points out, since Sapir also asserted that 'language defines our experience for us', we are presented by him with an extreme relativist position which makes even a comparison of experience impossible.

Benjamin Whorf continued and expanded the relativist orientation of Sapir. His view was that the grammars of different languages direct and shape the thought of the language users. Language is therefore a powerful force in the formation of the culture of any society, regulating its institutions, classifying its knowledge, and imposing on all a particular way of seeing things. Whorf asserts (De Cecco, 1966, p.71):

We dissect nature along lines laid down by our native language. The categories and types that we isolate from the world of phenomena we do not find there because they stare every observer in the face; on the contrary, the world is presented in a kaleidoscopic flux of impressions which has to be organised by our minds—and this means largely by the linguistic systems in our minds. We cut nature up, organise it into concepts, and ascribe significances as we do, largely because we are parties to an agreement to organise it in this way—an agreement that holds throughout our speech community and is codified in the patterns of our language. The agreement is of course an implicit and unstated one. BUT ITS TERMS ARE ABSOLUTELY OBLIGATORY; we cannot talk at all except by subscribing to the organisation and classification of data which the agreement decrees.

This theoretical outlook brings Whorf to the conclusion that no scientist can look at phenomena altogether impartially. It also brings him to formulate a new principle of relativity: 'that all observers are not led by the same physical evidence to the same picture of the universe unless their linguistic backgrounds are similar or can in some way be calibrated' (ibid.).

It must be stressed that the extreme relativism of Sapir's formula and of Whorf is not endorsed by all anthropologists. In this connection Lounsbury has to say that (p.10)

Not all linguists or cultural anthropologists however, either in Sapir's, Whorf's time or now, have been willing to see the common bases of human experience and the 'psychological unity of mankind' so subordinated to the superstructure of social, cultural and linguistic systems that they are denied an identification as fundamental and universal starting points for all such systems.

This accords with the Marxist view whose materialist conception of history applies to and finds confirmation in all cultures, in all societies irrespective of the differences between them.

It therefore goes further than Lounsbury whose formulation—'common bases of human experience and the "psychological unity of mankind" '—may be seen to have an affinity with notions of forces of production as a fundamental determinant of social relations and of language as a special characteristic of homo sapiens, as a distinct 'species being'. In its self-identification as a conception of history Marxism points also to social development, stages of which may be higher or lower. Cultures are therefore seen to be commensurable with each other by reference to a scale of development, and the same may be said of language. Stalin writes (1950, p.19):

We may assume that the rudiments of modern language already existed in hoary antiquity, before the epoch of slavery. It was a rather simple language, with a very meagre stock of words, but with a grammatical system—true, a primitive one, but a grammatical system nevertheless.

The further development of production, the appearance of classes, the introduction of writing, the rise of the state, which needed a more or less well-regulated correspondence for its administration, the development of trade, which needed a well-regulated correspondence still more, the appearance of the printing press, the development of literature—all these caused big changes in the development of language.

A specific of Marxist theory however, is that in class societies movement from one stage of social development to a new higher stage is brought about by class struggle. This being so, is it then supposed that language is in some way influenced by the class structure of a given society? There are two ways of facing this problem, both of which yield the same answer. The first is to point to the existence of classless societies before the emergence of private property and the state, and to the perspective of a classless society resulting from the establishment of socialism. Changes in language cannot be assumed to have been absent from the earlier epoch and must be assumed to be an inevitable part of future development. In the former case such changes must have accompanied the change from food gathering to domestication of animals and agriculture; in the latter from whatever technological changes socialism has in store for humanity. The second is to restate that class structure embodies relations of production, whereas it is the forces of production which are most potent in rendering old words obsolete, in begetting new words, and in changing the meanings of words which are retained. For this reason, vocabulary change can occur during the course of existence of a given social system, whereas the event of a change in class power is not, in itself, expected to result in the same kind of change.

Both ways of facing the problem of social class and language then, provide no reason for thinking that languages are class based. Stalin puts the matter thus (ibid., pp.13–14):

as long as capitalism exists the bourgeoisie and the proletariat will be bound together by every economic thread as parts of capitalist society . . . however sharp the class struggle may be, it cannot lead to the disintegration of society. Only ignorance of Marxism and complete failure to understand the nature of language could have suggested to some of our comrades the fairy tale about the disintegration of society, about class languages, and class grammars.

Language and deprivation

The languages available to capitalists and workers are the same. The availability of the language is not. And it is not, because the economic threads that bind workers to capitalists are such as to bring about for them an impoverishment of experience of life generally and therefore of language. Marx understood quite well the cultural and linguistic deprivation suffered by working-class children as part of their general exploitation. In a footnote to *Capital* (1926 edn, vol. I, p.285) he writes:

The degree of culture of these labour-powers must naturally be such as appears in the following dialogue with one of the commissioners: Jeremiah Haynes, age 12—'Four times four is 8; 4 fours are 16. A king is him that has all the money and gold. We have a King (told it is a Queen), they call her the Princess Alexandra. Told that she married the Queen's son. The Queen's son is the Princess Alexandra. A Princess is a man . . . [and so on].

Later in chapter XV (pp.436–7) he writes:

But the intellectual desolation artificially produced by converting immature human beings into mere machines for the fabrication of surplus-value. . . finally compelled even the English Parliament to make elementary education a compulsory condition to the productive employment of children under 14 years in every industry subject to the Factory Acts. . . .
Previous to the passing of the amended Factory Act in 1844, it happened, not infrequently, that the certificates of attendance at school were signed by the school master or school-mistress with a cross, as they themselves were unable to write.

And he goes on to quote the 'Report of Inspector of Factories, 31st October, 1858', 'In a second school I found the schoolroom 15 feet long and 10 feet wide, and counted in this space 75 children who were gabbling something unintelligible'.

Industrial development and its requirements, besides over a century of struggle since then by the working class and its allies, have wrought many and profound changes in the educational experience of the children of the working class. They have not so far, however, ended exploitation in England. There do appear, therefore, certain differences in language used by adult members as well as children of the working class as compared with that of adults and children from the so-called middle class.

It is to this area of enquiry that the sociological imagination and analysis of Basil Bernstein has been so fruitfully applied.

The educationalist witnesses and engages in the transmission of culture. He is supremely conscious of the interactions whereby children assume roles—considered as identities, as types or as members of institutions and social classes. He is therefore, quite ready to see speech codes as generated by forms of particular social relationships and finds special relevance in Bernstein's view which 'differs from and perhaps relativises Whorf, by asserting that . . . there will arise distinct linguistic forms—fashions of speaking—which induce in the speakers different ways of relating to objects and persons' (Bernstein, 1965, p.150). Not so relevant will appear Whorf's own principle of linguistic relativity. For whereas Bernstein looks for relativism within a culture, Whorf finds it between cultures. It should be noted that Bernstein is not himself critical of relativism as such.

There are, nevertheless, several advantages in the way that Basil Bernstein has brought educationalists to a study of both sociology and language. These advantages arise from a clear theoretical framework of ideas. To begin with his definition of role as 'a constellation of shared learned meanings' (p.152) brings back into focus an understanding that institutional roles such as teacher, and typed roles of an instrumental or expressive kind are modes of interaction— average patterns—wherein each datum is an identity corresponding more or less to what is a recognisable set of behaviours. Similarly in his formulation of the relationship between speech code and social process, 'the form of the social relation or—more generally—the social structure generates distinct linguistic forms or codes and these codes essentially transmit the culture and so constrain behaviour (p.144), structure and culture are shown to be dual aspects of societal interaction. Their unity is realised in language, in the speech codes generated by them.

We are led by Bernstein to consider how a social situation is expressed in speech. Since any one person has a number of roles— or at least a number of sub-roles in a role-set—he will prepare to choose from his stock of verbal expressions what to say in accordance with the currently active role. As a listener in the same social relation he will prepare also to receive, and to respond to, an expected level of lexical and syntactic choice. The speech used is, therefore, 'a consequence of the social relation'.

For socialisation this is of prime importance. It means that in the very act of trying to speak, a child is striving to make of himself a bearer of the subcultural meanings in force in his world. His role as it develops is given another form in his utterance of his needs, his intentions, his demands. Each generation must, in the first place, regenerate the speech systems giving expression to their subcultures. Every child has access, thus, to an appropriate speech code.

Bernstein distinguishes two types of code: a restricted code and an elaborated code. The former arises where the experience of the participants in a social relationship is so closely shared and exclusive that 'the need to verbalise intent' is reduced. Thus speech structure is simplified, the range of verbal alternatives is narrowed; extra-verbal expressions gain in importance, especially in denoting individual differences; the circumstances and manner of speech assume importance rather than the content; meanings tend to be 'descriptive or narrative rather than analytical or abstract'; articulation is imprecise; correct prediction by an observer of statements to be uttered is high. The characteristics of an elaborated code are in direct contrast: complex speech structure; wide range of alternatives; reduced importance of the extra-verbal; content matters more than manner or circumstance; analytical and abstract meanings are more likely.

By introducing a typology of meaning and models Bernstein is able to postulate 'formal sociological conditions' governing the elaborated and restricted speech codes. Meanings are universalistic if they are not germane only to particular situations, and if they 'are made explicit and are conventionalised through language' (p.157). But they are particularistic if the reverse is the case and if they 'relatively less conventionalised through language'.

So, an elaborated speech code can be universalistic in respect to its meanings, but, because it is possible (probable) that the purveyors of these meanings will be relatively few, can be particularistic in respect of its models. A restricted speech code will be particularistic in respect of its meaning but in respect of its models there are two possibilities. For the most part the model is universalistic but for a special case not only meaning but model too is particularistic. 'In this situation the individual is wholly constrained by the code. *He has access to no other*' (p.158).

It is important to understand that the speech codes are planning activities having existence only at the psychological level. But there inhere in the codes special social relationships. Social changes therefore must modify the codes which in turn change both their users and their meanings.

The educational consequences of the codes are far reaching; for the social, emotional and intellectual learning allowed by them are of different kinds. With an elaborated code a child is enabled to experience above all his separateness from others—his individuality. But the code has two forms of expression: (i) as a verbal elaboration of relations between persons; (ii) as a verbal elaboration between objects. Possession of either (i) or (ii) or both is possible. In any case he will have access also to a restricted code.

For the child with a restricted code, analysis and classification as well as synthesis and concept formation in relation to experience are inhibited. The speech of others is not specially significant and his own speech lacks motivation to develop. The speech of a child with a restricted code cannot be used therefore to signal his states of mind. 'Logical sequence and stress' are inhibited by such speech; redundancy of expression and repetition are promoted. But this kind of speech corresponds to social relations which generated it. It is therefore not inferior to an elaborated code even though society evaluates differently the subcultures generating them.

Using tools generally worked with in educational research in Britain, Bernstein proves by a comparison between verbal and non-verbal intelligence quotients that the linguistic codes are not simply a function of the native ability of children. The meanings inherent in the codes are social, as are the models from whom they are learnt. Both meaning and model which constrain the learnings of the child are there for him first of all in the family.

But the complex of roles in a family is closely governed by its social class status. Since the family mediates the subcultural orientations of the social class, social class is an index though an extremely crude one, of the speech code to be expected. Children from middle-class families are likely to have access to an elaborated code as well as a restricted code; children from working-class families are likely to carry only a restricted code.

With regard to educability at school, the experience of two children may consequently be in contrast. For the middle-class child, school may constitute development. But because the social relationship and the symbolism change at school for the working-class child, it can involve discontinuity and a tendency to alienate him from his kin. The heightening of teachers' sensitivity to their own roles in the classroom is therefore an important educational aim.

Now at the outset of his closely reasoned argument 'A sociolinguistic approach to social learning (1965)' Bernstein states 'the thesis to be put forward here rests on the work of Vygotsky and Luria'. Certainly Luria in his lectures on *The Role of Speech in the Regulation of Normal and Abnormal Behaviour* (1961) emphasises the importance of a child's relationship with adults in his overall development. His view is that a young child is socially bound most significantly with his mother and that language between them has three main processes: naming things, giving orders, explaining. When a child names objects he is organising acts of perception and he is at the same time organising acts of deliberate attention. A child repeats orders given to him and in doing so he retains traces of verbal instruction. From that he goes on to formulate his own wishes and intentions in externalised speech. This is followed developmentally by internalised speech, purposive memory, and deliberate activity. This process, 'the process in which functions previously shared between two persons gradually change into complicated systems in the mind . . . forms the essence of human higher mental activity' (1967, p.3). With regard to meaning, when a mother names and points she is helping the child to do the same. But when he names and points he alters the relative strength of the stimuli around him and his behaviour is bound to be modified by the new way in which he sees his environment.

This view of Luria follows faithfully Vygotsky's, that once the two separate elements of growth (intellect and speech) meet, further intellectual development is determined by language, that is, by the linguistic tools of thought and by the socio-cultural experience of the child: 'With the development of inner speech and of verbal thought, the nature of development itself changes from biological to socio-historical' (1962, p.51).

There is therefore agreement concerning the formative significance of societal pressures and their mediation through speech (though not through speech only) on the emergence of identities.

Nevertheless there is much in Bernstein's scheme which cannot be said to rest on the ideas of Vygotsky and Luria. The references to intelligence quotients mark one difference. In these is implied an acceptance of the proposition that intelligence is genetically deter-mined—is itself not influenced by experience—and may be measured at any time. 'Children who have access to different speech systems. . . adopt quite different social and intellectual procedures despite a common potential' (Bernstein, 1965, p.150). It is clear that this view runs contrary to Vygotsky's and to that of Luria. The former regards word-meaning as the essential unit of linguistic analysis, points to different levels of generality and abstraction of word-meanings and insists that intellectual development depends upon their acquisition—especially from parents, teachers and older children. For example: 'The lines along which a complex [a variation in a type of thinking] develops are predetermined by the meaning a given word already has in the language of adults' (Vygotsky, 1962, p.66). And again 'In the higher mental functions and processes emerging during the child's cultural development formal discipline must play a part that is does not play in the more elementary processes' (p.97).

On the difference with Luria it is enough to recall his experiment with the twins, in *Speech and the Development of the Mental Processes in the Child*. The second aspect of this experiment involved the subjection of the more retarded sibling to a programme of language instruction, which, after a short period left him in advance of his brother intellectually.

A second difficulty arises from the lack of consistency in Bernstein's analysis of the social conditions which give rise to an elaborated code. Speech models for such a code are said to be 'incumbents of the specialised positions located in the system of social stratification' (Bernstein, 1965, p.158). Since, however, 'In principle this is not necessary but it is likely to be the case' (ibid.), we are obviously not at the root of the matter.

Earlier in the paper the condition of the social relationship giving rise to an elaborated code is defined as that which impels members of a group, 'to select . . . a verbal arrangement which closely fits specific referents. This situation will arise where the intent of the person cannot be taken for granted' (p.156). Plainly, one social relationship will inhibit intent being taken for granted and therefore promote verbal specificity, another social relationship will act in the opposite direction. But the social relationship engendering these qualities is not defined by saying that it exists.

Other stated features of the elaborated code, or of the social relationship generating it, likewise do not meet this requirement (pp.156–7, 160–1).

> The code will facilitate the verbal transmission of the individual's unique experience . . . and elaborated code facilitates verbal transmission of individualised or personal symbols . . . induces in its speakers a sensitivity to the implications of separateness. . . .
>
> An elaborated code . . . becomes a facility for transmitting individuated verbal responses. . . . The concept of self unlike the concept of self in a restricted code will be verbally differentiated.

In none of these formulations is there a description of 'The form of the social relation [that] regulates the options which the speakers take up.' (p.151). What is to be noted, however, is the recurring motif which brings into prominence the problem of the relationship of the individual to the group.

It should be remembered here that in respect of the restricted code, the form of the social relationship which engenders it is very clearly defined as being, 'based upon a common set of closely-shared identifications and expectations self-consciously held . . . the social relationship will be of an inclusive kind. The speech here is refracted through a common cultural identity' (p.155).

What has to be explained therefore are the conditions under which identifications and expectations become less closely shared, less inclusive, and as a consequence of which speech therefore becomes less refractable through a common cultural identity.

Incidentally this is also the key approach to the way in which the individual may be seen to stand in opposition to the group. Individuality cannot be said to derive from itself, verbally or otherwise. As Bernstein indicates, personality grows in accordance with the sub-cultural complex of expectations as they are mediated by the specific interactions engaging an actor, Theoretically therefore, the variations made possible by the special characteristics of genetic origin can only be arrived at by eliminating the immediately relevant, socially evolved, historical conditions of his experience. And such a procedure would have to take account also of the selection exercised by the force of cultural pressure on the enormous range of possibilities inherent in any human being. On this view, individuation and the way in which it manifests itself expresses a social relation. It does not determine a social relation.

That which makes necessary awareness of separability is the fact of separation. And this occurs when a member of one group belongs also to another. Individuality is seen therefore to involve a claim on the part of a member of a group to allow his role therein to become latent and to make his role elsewhere an active one. Awareness of self arises when the need to advance this claim makes itself felt. Such a process cannot occur without the existence of, or the possibility of the existence of, another group and a socially conditioned affinity towards it on the part of the person(s) concerned. Present-day preoccupation with the individual is here seen to be an outcome of the social division of labour as it is realised in the differentiation of institutions for the accomplishment of socially necessary purposes.

The production of goods in industrial society for example, involves the separation of at least one bread-winner from his home for much of the day. Industrial society also involves the attendance of children at school and therefore their separation from the family. A wife-mother who, say, is an active worker for the Labour Party declares her separability from the family in addressing herself to the latter role. Given therefore a family in which the husband-father is the main bread-winner, two children aged eleven and thirteen at school, and a wife-mother active in the Labour Party, there arises, continually, an acute need for each member of that family to be seen as separable from it. On the other hand, at work, at school, in the Labour Party ward branch, there will have to be an accepted separability in order that familial roles may be fulfilled.

In addition to the separability of a group's members, induced by their roles elsewhere, there is also the pressure upon each group to accommodate to the meanings and purposes at work in other groups. In the case of the family, the type, the terms and conditions of employment of the male spouse, the type and level of education of the children, the nature of the activities engaged in by the Labour Party ward branch, cannot but be absorbed in family routines and expectations. But this only happens in so far as this group validates, blocks or gives way to, inhibits or assists, dominates or becomes subordinate to each member's activity elsewhere. Individuality is, therefore, the personal bringing to a group, of meanings derived from other social interactions by one of that group's members. It is conditioned by membership elsewhere. Distortion of an understanding of the social relationship is induced to the extent that separateness is overstressed and membership underestimated. This view is fully in accord with that of Marx in the *Theses on Feuerbach*: 'The essence of man is no abstraction inherent in each separate individual. In its reality it is the ensemble [aggregate] of social relations' (1969 edn, p.285).

Thus, it is the social relation of multiple role which makes necessary the linguistic transmission of its characteristics: relatively sharp specificity; explicit formulation and declaration of intent; a wide range of meanings; a likelihood of abstract and analytical thought.

The importance of separation-membership-elsewhere has been shown in the Luria experiment with twins. As is well known, faced with the problem of helping the language and general development of a pair of twins whose mutual but restrictive support was reinforced by keeping them together, Luria proposed their separation from each other. It is doubtful whether progress would have been as rapid as it was had they been placed with toys and apparatus in separate rooms to play alone as individuals. But by setting them in different groups of children each of the twins was faced with membership of another group. The outcome was (Luria and Yudovich, 1971, p.69),

Removal of the twin situation led to remarkable progress . . . .
Once included in a situation of speech communication, the twins came not only to use speech for active communication but also the boundaries of their understanding were significantly widened. . . . After only three to four months of the experiment we could not easily single out our twins from the other children.

Moreover, and perhaps of greater import for our understanding of individuality and inner-group relationships, the relationship of the twins to each other, that is to say, the relationship within the group, was radically changed as a result of the new connections formed outside it. When the twins were placed together there was an observed abundance of speech formerly absent. Complex speech accompanied play activities. Two important functions of speech generated were: (i) orientations of the children to their games; (ii) analysis of their play situation.

For the development of a critique of Bernstein's general thesis it is necessary at this point to turn to an essay entitled 'Education cannot compensate for society' (1972). In this essay the literature concerning compensatory education is listed and the underlying assumptions of the movement examined.

It is pointed out that despite the material inadequacy of many primary and secondary schools, despite the open and hidden streaming in schools where 'lower expectations and motivation of both teachers and taught' (p.106) are typical, there is the false assumption that we do offer 'an initial satisfactory educational environment'. Attention is consequently diverted from our failure in the schools towards families and children. Labels like cultural deprivation epitomise this critical orientation. In themselves these labels evoke from teachers a depreciation of certain children, of their parents, their culture and its symbols. Their cultural devaluation brings about a severe discontinuity of meaning for such children. Structurally, they are alienated from their families and communities. In their identification as being deprived their parents are defined as being inadequate.

Having said this, Bernstein then tries to show how schools can compensate for society by bringing 'parents within the educational experience of the schoolchild' (p.107). If the parents can be brought to help the children in what ways they can, if the content of the learning is drawn from the child's subcultural background—such discontinuity, devaluation and alienation will be avoided.

Bernstein makes it quite clear that his reason for emphasising the socialising force of educational practice is to clarify his position on language. Mistaken inferences from his writings have to be corrected. And the major error of his interpreters has been to 'divorce the use of language from the substratum of cultural meanings which are initially responsible for the language use. The concept "restricted code", to describe working-class speech, has been equated with "linguistic deprivation" or even with the "non-verbal" child' (p.109).

To clarify the difference between the two codes a contrast is drawn between language use which is context-bound and language use which is less context-bound. An example of the former usage is by working-class five-year-olds who verbalise a ball-playing window-breaking sequence of four pictures, in such a way that reference to the pictures remains necessary to understand the story. But middle-class five-year-olds make understanding possible without reference to the pictures. What is critical is the use of nouns and pronouns: working-class children used two nouns and fourteen pronouns; middle-class children used thirteen nouns and six pronouns.

Another contrast is between one mother who elaborates, in controlling her child, 'rules and reasons for rules and their consequences' (ibid., p.111) and another mother who deals only with particular acts.

Universalism as a quality of language, in the first comparison, releases the story-teller from the context; the second comparison expresses a degree of generality or of law-governing behaviour. Particularism as a quality of language binds the story-teller to a context and inhibits this same process of generalisation which is the foundation of rule-making.

Research usually indicates that middle-class children 'are oriented towards receiving and offering universalistic meanings, whereas [others] are oriented towards particularistic meanings'. This arises from the fact that, 'The social classes differ in terms of the *contexts* which evoke certain linguistic realisations'. But working-class parents, 'are *not* linguistically deprived, nor are their children'.

Particularism, universalism and revolution

Some critics of compensatory education go further than Bernstein's correction of his first formulations. They attack compensatory education as well as the notions of cultural and linguistic deprivation, but they go on from that to attack also the validity of difference in subcultures as being responsible for low education attainment. In their paper, *The Myth of the Restricted Code* (1971), Byrne and Williamson investigate whether the causes of differences in the rate of staying on at school to sixteen in 1968, as a measure of educational attainment in that year, are to be found in subcultural influences including linguistic elements like restricted or elaborated codes, or whether they are to be discovered rather in the influences of resource, provision, and high/low social class representation. The conclusions are that the latter group of factors are the major determinants of attainment and that policies seeking solutions to educational problems which do not recognise this are either naïve or deceptive. The major alternatives to be chosen from are (i) policies such as were developed in the Plowden Report which orient themselves to alleged cultural deficiencies in the working class and their families; (ii) policies which centre on 'redistribution of material resources'. Byrne and Williamson are plainly for redistribution.

It will be seen that the remarks to be made concerning Bernstein's own attack on compensatory education are directly applicable here. But, before going on to that, it should be pointed out that no myth has in fact been exposed. What has been shown is that low educational attainments exist where there is a poverty of educational facilities. But low educational attainment as such has not been defined by Byrne and Williamson. What is provided is a measure of educational attainment—not at all the same thing. The non-existence of variations in verbal power, both oral and written, would have to be shown in quite another way, on the basis of work with children in school. Herein lies the strength of the concept of the speech codes. Teachers who work with children in primary, secondary modern and comprehensive schools experience what may be classified as restricted and elaborated speech codes. At the same time however, since they wish children to learn, they cannot accept that aspect of Bernstein's self-professed relativism which makes the codes, not extremes on a continuum, but parallel learning processes.

The relativism may be breached in another way. The cultural deprivation may be seen to be, not an outcome of familial inadequacy but the result of a heritage of neglect, the very outcome of the poverty of provision, as well as of poverty in general, complained of by Byrne and Williamson. Looked at in this way, a policy of positive discrimination may be a meagre reform but one operating in the right direction.

The retort must be, surely, 'Not enough!' Enough, however, can be accomplished only by the transformation of society—something which depends upon the abolition of capitalism. Are Byrne and Williamson for this? At the outset of the paper there is a whisper of Marx. But it is Weber who is called upon to explain (Byrne and Williamson, 1971, pp.6–7):

> The perspective on social stratification on the other hand which
> has been central to Sociology from Marx and Weber onwards
> and which has been carefully neglected by educational
> sociologists is that which focuses directly on the distribution
> and control of, and access to goods or resources in the
> determination of life chances of individuals and groups.
> Central to this notion of stratification is the notion of 'power'.
> As Weber puts it: ' "classes", "status groups", and "Parties"
> are phenomena of the distribution of power within a
> community'.

Weber, of course speaks for himself. Marx, whose primary focus is on exploitation and on political power as the guarantee of its continuance, is concerned with the dynamics of a class struggle to expropriate the expropriators. Weber's measure—the dimensions of life chances for individuals or groups—can, of course, be construed to include exploitation. From Marx's analysis awareness of exploitation and of its specifically capitalist form becomes inescapable, with palpable consequences for the capitalist system. Similarly, it is possible to construe from the paper of Byrne and Williamson that they want this transformation of the social system. It is also possible to infer that the reallocation of resources on a scale great enough to do what is necessary in education may be done in some other way.

Now in one respect Bernstein's notion of context-bound language has a parallel with a key concept used by Luria in classifying the speech of children. This is the concept of synpraxic speech. For Luria as for Vygotsky, the word has a basic function, not only because it indicates a corresponding object in the external world, but also because 'it abstracts and isolates the necessary signal, generalises the perceived signals and relates them to certain categories' (Luria and Yudovitch, 1971, p.23). It follows then that when a child's words cannot be used by him outside the activity or in the absence of the objects, the basic function referred to is not operative for the child. Speech then which interlocks a word with the activity or object and which fails to separate the sign from its referent, remains 'a fragment of a concrete-active situation' (p.50) and is called synpraxic speech.

Here the resemblance between Bernstein's particularism and Luria's synpraxis ends. For Bernstein the fact that children's speech is likely to be context-bound, particularistic, of a restricted code implies no inferiority. The children with access only to a restricted code are merely different from those who have access also to an elaborated code. Since they have a different subculture with different meanings their social learning has to be different and the linguistic bearers of meanings must therefore likewise be different.

But for Vygotsky and Luria synpraxic speech is a lower stage of linguistic development. Until the word is freed from its context mental development is itself confined, the scope of meanings is severely limited and social intercourse drastically reduced.

Any reluctance to label the working class or its attributes as inferior is certainly to be applauded, and especially those who are committed to the emancipation of that class must welcome this reluctance. But a prospect of emancipation implies a consciousness of current exploitation. To expose the various ways in which the proletariat is short-changed and kept subordinate is not to label it as inferior—it is to designate the modes of its oppression. Indeed the crucial leap in the consciousness of the worker to a universalistic orientation is that of his self-knowledge—not merely as a fitter or as a bricklayer, not even as a wage-earner (which is a higher order of generality)—but as a member of one class, standing, by virtue of a certain relationship to the means of production, against another class.

This is to say that in the social relationship between the bourgeoisie and proletariat there inhere patterns of action and interaction which determine the nature of meanings available to the consciousness of the members of these classes. Unless the worker reaches a given level of class consciousness, unless he grasps certain concepts relevant to the social dynamics affecting his status, unless he enters deliberately into those patterns of interaction typical of class struggle, his conditions of work and life must generate particularistic orientations which must be expressed in the language he uses.

Marx offers major insights into particularism/universalism when he discusses the dialectical connection between concrete and abstract labour, between use-value and value, between commodities as equivalents to each other and the money commodity. Above all, he demonstrates this in his description of the social division of labour which reflects the division of labour specific to any one factory: 'The separation of the intellectual powers of production from the manual labourer and the conversion of these powers into the might of capital over labour' (1926 edn, vol. I, p.462). The capitalist stands, however, in relation to production as witness to its entire process and in relation to the market as witness of the economic process as a whole. Thus, his economic status has its complement in roles whose meanings have a greater universality than have his clerks and his overseers, his managers and his scientists. It appears then that particularism and universalism have their different levels of oppositeness (antithesis). The capitalist has a higher order of universality of meaning and role than any of his employees in the occupational hierarchy that contrasts manual with non-manual wage- and salary-earners. But all this is true only as long as the capitalist system itself is taken as given—as long as the status/role arrangement of capitalism is not challenged. Once there arises a consciousness of the possibility of a system which might supersede capitalism, once this consciousness is institutionalised in trade unions and political parties, then on a higher plane the capitalist class is reduced to the historical particularism which demands that its own era should be everlasting. The proletariat, on the other hand, insisting that a new order must be inaugurated, has to orient itself to a new order of universalism, must learn to see capitalism as a passing phenomenon, must master the ideology which will sustain its revolutionary purpose and found a new socialist order. A complex of meanings of this order cannot be carried in a restricted speech code.

It is fundamentally on these grounds that there can be proclaimed the superiority of the working class over the capitalist class. And with this in mind it is unnecessary to search for formulae intended to hide the poverty of the working class, or to label that poverty as being merely a quality of a different social relation which requires a different learning process which in turn needs a different linguistic code. Under capitalism the working class is exploited. Its economic alienation (i) from decision-making concerning the ends of production; (ii) from the means of production; (iii) from the product itself results in deprivation of many kinds. Not the least of these is educational deprivation.

If then the pervading quality of life of the working class expresses its exploitation, is this quality of its social relation omitted from the language used by its members? If Bernstein is correct, that is to say if a restricted code of speech with its characteristics of being context-bound, of limiting analytical and abstract expressions, of inhibiting individuation, is in no sense linguistic deprivation, then it follows that what is true of the quality of a social relation need not be true of its linguistic expression. This however, stands directly opposite to the starting point of Bernstein's entire thesis: that the speech code is itself a quality of the social relation and is the major communicative bearer of its meanings.

The educational practice advocated by Bernstein shows his implicit realisation that a restricted code is an inferior one, for he is concerned that children who are without an elaborated code should be helped to acquire one. True he insists on reducing alienation from, and conflict with, such children's subcultural setting and suggests a number of techniques to avoid culture-shock and discontinuity: securing parents' co-operation, awakening teachers to working-class children's cognitive and value orientations, making curriculum more meaningful. But the direction pointed to, is none the less, towards freedom from the context in linguistic performance, towards elaboration of speech code.

It would be mistaken to emphasise the adequacy of speech code in relation to a home background, or to a neighbourhood. The principle here seems to be that such emphasis duly restricts the sociologist to description and analysis, that is, fosters an ideal of a value-free sociology. First, it may be said, any consideration of adequacy cannot but be evaluative, is part of analysis, and goes beyond description. Second, description and analysis which do not take into account an institution's or a subculture's linkage with society as a whole must be incomplete. Third, a statement of adequacy, if it omits reference to probable future contingencies inherent in social change is not comprehensive enough to sustain its own worth. Fourth, the operation of such a principle would not be supportive of Bernstein's general position since this is overtly prescriptive and therefore evaluative.

It is to be concluded therefore that if one type of linguistic equipment facilitates better performance than another in the school situation and prepares more successfully for a wider range of social probabilities, it is not merely different but better. As Hobhouse knew so well, relativism is to be challenged as much in sociology as in ethics.

What emerges from this is that the value of the distinction between the two codes lies fundamentally in its exposure of a particular process of social control whose current is in the direction of continued exploitation, i.e. deprivation, of the working class. Once the different subcultural meanings are brought into relation with each other, their connections shown, this becomes quite clear. To treat the subcultures as separate entities, each generating itself is to forget that there is a cultural unity of a kind that—until some sort of social revolution is consummated—gives each subculture a special meaning for every other subculture and that each such meaning is a quality of that cultural unity. Capitalism must have, besides its capitalist class, its working class as well.

This points to severe limits on a policy—easily derived from Bernstein's prescription—which sees as the main solution to educational poverty the use of subcultural orientations which include diffuseness of thought, context-bound expression, low educational levels, poor conceptual development, absence of generality in thinking.

The relativism of Bernstein obtains simultaneous support and challenge from Eric Midwinter's account of the Liverpool EPA

project in *Priority Education* (1972). Midwinter insists that the term
deprivation has deep meaning in its application to the lives of some
working-class children: 'Do people have to be luridly told, every
month or so, that children are living multi-deprived existences . . . ?'
(p.26). But he moves from this through the formula, 'It is not too
polemical to imply that to the injury of a deprived existence, is added
the insult of an alien educational system', to the proposition that we
should have a system of educational institutions corresponding to a
variety of subcultures. 'Perhaps different sorts of areas required
different educational systems. The educational servicing of a multi-
variant society with a singular system leads to schools which fail to
relate to the experience of their pupils and their catchment area' (p.13).
Thus the notion of compensatory education as a means of correcting
or offsetting deprivation is replaced with a new formula (pp.80; 105):

The feeling of the project team had hardened in favour of a
differentiated, rather than a compensatory, form of education in
the E.P.A. . . . . This heightened regard for schools, differing in
pattern and content as their catchment areas prescribed, evolved,
vis-à-vis the establishment of a more definitive view of the
community school, as one in which school and community
interlocked closely for mutual benefit. This implied that the
community school must vary according to the dictates of its
surrounds. Thus, on both grounds, the idea of an EPA
Community School, distinct in character from the other schools,
became clearer.

And through the actual operation of school-home links in the
first year, we also began to see the problem more lucidly in such
educational terms as the interacting effect of neighbourhood
and school on the child. We began to talk of complementary,
rather than 'compensatory education' with the school
endeavouring to establish rapport with the values of home
and community, rather than, if only by implication, opposing
them.

Now the values of home and community in the urban slum, as
far as they have been discerned by Midwinter, have produced no
solutions to the deprivation experienced by its inhabitants. If the
school is to be merely a complement of the EPA it can be assumed
that there will be no room for the kind of ideology that may lead to
a radical alteration of the situation. Relativism sees a milieu for what
it is and recognises the necessity of its difference from others: 'The

lesson of the suburban school is that it identifies with its environs'. This leads on to the proposition that teacher-training be overtly structured in the direction of producing specific subcultural pedagogical types—as if this is not now broadly an aspect of teacher supply. 'There seems no reason why, as well as the conventional divisions by chronology or subject found in the colleges of education, there should not be sociological divisions catering for the requirements of especial communal typologies' (p.125). The totality of these propositions make for the prospect of a multivariant society which includes its EPAs, with a variety of community schools corresponding with class and status divisions and teacher training arrangements to suit.

Midwinter's reforming zeal cannot, however, accept this outcome of his own logic (pp.22; 146).

[The community schools'] long term purpose is to equip the
critical parent, worker, consumer and citizen of the next
generation in the hope that generation might respond
creatively to the challenge of deprivation.

I regard this somersault in the teacher's role, from, by and
large, supporting the status quo, more than hitherto, helping the
child to criticise it, as the chief barrier between the idea of
community education and its realisation.

Despite the denials, the conditions defining the community schools impose severe limits on the possibility that there will emerge ideas of a quality, and in quantity, sufficient to bring about the desired change. The conditions cannot but lock the community school—in the EPA at any rate—together with its community, in the embrace of those social relationships which themselves generate deprivation. These conditions seem to be:

(1) that the solutions to the problems of the community are to come as a result of the re-education along lines indicated by the EPA team;

(2) that the collective accumulating wisdom of the working class, as institutionalised in its trade union and political organisations be largely ignored as irrelevant;

(3) the fostering of anti-intellectualism in the schools—especially among teachers (see remarks on language-learning, algebra, literature) of the EPAs;

(4) that a world outlook (world geography for example) give way to a restricted neighbourhood outlook;

(5) that analyses so far made of the causes of deprivation—
especially if they involve something in the nature of sustained study—
have no relevance, since their relevance is not immediately understood, to the multi-deprivation of the EPAs.

With regard to this last item it is especially necessary to refute the
stated consensus of ignorance: 'the persistent wail [from the uni-
versities] that "We don't really know how children are deprived, so
how can we help them?" God knows that it is true, but we can't idle
away the years, doing nothing about self-evident glaring situations'
(ibid., p.51). Well, at least Marxism knows about the mechanisms of
exploitation. For these to be replaced with other mechanisms
requires quite other means—even in education—than those expounded by Midwinter.

An alternative policy is the development of an educated working
class, whatever dangers this may bring for capitalism. For this it is
supremely important that teachers should be concerned not with the
promotional social-mobility possibilities seen to inhere in educational attainment, but with the intellectual development of all
children. No one doubts the need to use the environment and the
experience of children in educational endeavour, but understanding
of their environment, insight into their experience cannot be accomplished without words and concepts which may not be, normally,
part of their immediate life-situation.

Language and education

It is in this connection that the ideas of Vygotsky on thought and
language are important. For Vygotsky sees the school as that agency
of socialisation whose special role it is to promote conceptual
development (1962, p.92. My italics).

In perceiving some of our own acts in a generalising fashion,
we isolate them from our total mental activity and are thus
enabled to focus on this process as such. . . . In this way,
becoming conscious of our operations and viewing each as a
process of a certain kind—such as remembering and imagining—
lead to their mastery. *School instruction induces the generalising
kind of perception* and thus plays a decisive role in making the
child conscious of his own mental processses.

Vygotsky's work on language is preponderantly psychological.
Nevertheless it is of significance sociologically because it provides

the elements of a strategy for teaching—itself a social process. The principles inspiring this are:

(1) that the irreducible unit of language is word-meaning;

(2) that word-meanings have different orders of generality;

(3) that language is of central importance in the development of intelligence.

As to how socialising processes are facilitated by language Vygotsky's ideas stand in contrast with those of Piaget. Piaget, wrote that (quoted in Vygotsky, 1962, p.14):

> from the genetic point of view one must start from the child's activity in order to understand his thought and his activity is unquestionably egocentric and egotistic. The social instinct in well defined form develops late. The first critical period in this respect occurs towards the age of seven or eight.

Piaget's view is that thought and speech follow a common path from autistic to socialised speech—from subjective fantasy to the logic of relationships. Vygotsky's hypothesis reverses the order of the process. 'The true development of thinking is not from the individual to the socialised, but from the social to the individual' (p.20). The earliest speech is essentially social. Even egocentric speech is social because this represents internalisation of social behaviour. 'Egocentric speech splinters off from general social speech, and in time leads to inner speech which serves both autistic and logical thinking' (p.19).

This view has relevance for the general theory of socialisation. It indicates that a child is not biologically an asocial organism only to be socialised by the normative, cognitive, historically given pressures mediated by his first primary group. He is, biologically, a social animal in the first place. But this is insufficient for full social growth —growth which feeds by way of internalising the norms, and acquiring the knowledge peculiar to his time and place of living.

Against Piaget's genetic temporal sequences Vygotsky looks for cause and effect. Whereas Piaget claims the right to make his own arbitrary choices, 'We have chosen the sociological idiom but we emphasise that there is nothing exclusive about this—we reserve the right to return to the biological explanation of child thought' (quoted in Vygotsky, 1962, p.21), Vygotsky insists that 'a need can only be truly satisfied through a certain adaptation to reality. Moreover, there is no such thing as adaptation for the sake of adaptation. It is always directed by needs' (ibid.).

The reality of course is the life-situation of the child. Vygotsky shows, experimentally, that egocentric speech serves the child's rational activity, his purposeful actions, his problem-solving and his planning.

The sources of thought and speech, according to Vygotsky, are two separate genetic roots: pre-intellectual speech, pre-linguistic thought. At about two however, 'the curves of thought and speech meet and intiate a new form of behaviour . . . [the child] seems to have discovered the symbolic function of words, speech enters the intellectual phase' (p.43).

Although external speech through a series of stages gives rise to inner soundless speech—a form of thinking, the emergence of intellectual speech does not mean that thought and language are always and necessarily connected, even in adults. According to Vygotsky (p.51), 'there is a vast area of thought not related to speech [practical intellect] and there are speech forms not connected with thought'.

However, once verbal thought begins to develop in the child, 'the nature of development itself changes from biological to socio-historical. . . . The problem of thought and language thus extends beyond natural science and becomes the focal problem of historical human psychology, i.e. social-psychology' (p.51).

If we can accept the notions that (i) the meaning(s) embraced by any concept are derived from the cognitive and normative patterns in force in a given field of social relations at a given time—i.e. that the content of any given concept is social in nature—and that (ii) the conceptualisation itself is a psychological process, then Vygotsky's study of the relation of language to concept formation is of key importance to teachers. On the basis of studies of more than 300 children, adolescents and adults, the following principal findings were arrived at:

(1) the process eventually resulting in concept formation begins in earliest childhood;

(2) but the psychological basis of concept formation is completed only at puberty;

(3) before this, embryonic concept formations perform similar functions to those of the genuine concepts to come;

(4) a true concept is formed when the intellect operates to bring together all the elementary mental functions in a specific combination. 'This operation is guided by the use of words as the means of

actively centering attention, of abstracting certain traits, synthesising them and symbolising them by a sign' (ibid.).

In his analysis of learning at school Vygotsky criticises the theoretical separation of instruction from development because the analysis of learning 'is thus reduced to determining the developmental level that various functions must reach for instruction to become feasible' (p.94). He also criticises identification of development and instruction. His assessment of a third view, that development has two aspects—maturation and learning—is that this has distinct advantages over the other two. His own view is that mental development 'unfolds in a continuous interaction with the controls of instruction' (p.101). Instruction usually precedes development. Indeed, 'the only good kind of instruction is that which marches ahead of development and leads it' (p.104). Although the data available to Vygotsky supports strongly the existence of sensitive periods, 'the optimum timing for instruction in a given subject is not purely biological; there is a dependence on co-operation with adults and on instruction'. Teaching such operations that need awareness and control, 'maximally furthers development of higher psychological functions while they are maturing'. And for such teaching the school years are optimum periods. A teaching strategy therefore should not regard as necessary that the psychological foundations for instruction should precede it.

In working out his own theories of the relationship between instruction and development, Vygotsky, besides investigating the teaching of social science, natural science, arithmetic and grammar, has some illuminating remarks to make on writing. Writing constitutes a second degree of symbolisation: in learning to write the child must replace words by images of words. 'In conversation every sentence is prompted by a motive. . . . It does not have to be consciously directed—the dynamic of the situation takes care of that.' Regular and frequent provision of opportunities to write involves the creation of situations for speech without immediate respondents and may be 'addressed to an absent or imaginary person or to no one in particular'. It is this abstract quality—abstract in terms of distance from the semantic referent and abstract possibly in terms of the writing's content—which is the major difficulty in getting children to engage in writing.

In extension of the formula for individuation used in the critique of Bernstein, it may be said then that writing is an activity whose practice separates the member from the group. (The amanuensis is a special case.) Sociologically it enables a variety of reference groups to be considered, it stimulates examination of beliefs, attitudes and roles, without direct pressure from significant others, it facilitates re-orientation to primary group complexes, it exercises individuation.

On the psychological level Vygotsky states that writing requires 'deliberate analytical action' (p.99) and demands conscious work because of the relationship to inner speech: oral speech before inner speech, inner speech before written speech. Grammatically however, inner speech is in a way exactly opposite to written speech. The former, since the subject of thought is always known, is reduced almost to predication, whereas in the latter the syntax is deployed to the fullest extent: 'the change from the maximally compact inner speech to maximally detailed written speech requires deliberate structuring of the web of meaning' (p.100).

It will be readily seen therefore, that whilst explicit oral statement has a necessary part to play in stimulating thought and in the preparation for writing, the practice of writing itself (like the study of grammar) helps the child to rise to higher levels of speech development and of mental development. If this is the case moreover, trends in education to demote literacy in favour of oracy is not only harmful to mental development, but is likely, in the long run, to have a negative influence on the very oracy it is aimed to promote.

For our purpose, that of exploring the interconnection of social process, especially in education, with language—it is not necessary to follow Vygotsky's fascinating exposition concerning degrees of generality as a measure of relationship between concepts, or his proofs of transfer of abstract thinking from one area of knowledge to another. Highly relevant however, since they have linguistic expression and find their interplay especially in the classroom is the contrast he draws between spontaneous concepts and scientific concepts. Spontaneous concepts are derived from face-to-face meetings and from concrete situations. A scientific concept demands mediation in reference to its object. This is a more exact way of saying that some concepts may be learned inductively arising from oft-repeated experience with the matter to be generalised about. Other concepts however, can only be learned if they are systematically taught. What Vygotsky points out is that spontaneous concepts must have reached a certain level for successful absorption of scientific concepts. This is not a one-way street though. Successful absorption of scientific concepts speeds up spontaneous concept formation. One implication for us is that skilful teaching has its significance not only for what goes on in the classroom, but also for an understanding of direct experience elsewhere.

Another implication for us is the possibility of reassessing our view of the relationship between what sociologists call particularistic and universalistic orders of meaning. Marx showed how the concrete and the abstract (in the case of labour) exist as two antithetical but interrelated and necessary aspects of the same social phenomenon Bernstein, like most sociologists, makes of particularism and universalism two antithetical but distinct and separate categories. Vygotsky returns us, in his treatment of spontaneous and scientific concept formation, and their dynamic interaction, to a view more like that of Marx.

It is convenient now to examine one more theoretical issue in the Bernstein model. The thesis is that some children have access to an elaborated code and a restricted code: other children have access only to a restricted code. But the different codes are said to be generated by different social structures and subcultures. Yet it is the former group of children whose educational/familial experience is a continuous unity and the latter group of children who experience two orders of meaning. Clearly there must be a crucial difference between the restricted code of the elaborate code users and the restricted code of the others.

Vygotsky's insight, the comparison between 'maximally compact inner speech' and 'maximally detailed written speech' (p.100) is helpful here. For it is the former which has relevance for conversational situations especially where the participants share an area of identifications and expectations. Shortened externalised speech corresponding to the compact inner speech and accompanied by non-verbal elements of communication may be highly predictable (a key characteristic of a restricted code) but may, at the same time, very well refer to highly specific, abstract meanings (characteristics of an elaborated code).

There are two suggestions here; (i) that the linguistic expressions used in situations arising from one status and behaviour complex cannot be an intermittent quality of another greatly different status and behaviour complex; (ii) that a shortened version of an elaborated code must be distinguished from a restricted code.

Finally we should return to the problem of the speech codes and their significance for educational strategies. It would appear, if we are to take Vygotsky's work into account, that reasons for discontinuity between two parallel, concurrent orders of meaning experienced by a child may include a lower level of conceptual development on the part of parents or of other models outside school. But the linguistic expression of this discontinuity cannot be removed directly by reference to the codes.

Two mutually exclusive strategies seem to present themselves. A relativist strategy will reduce the discontinuity in the short term by means of restricting the level and range of conceptual endeavour—but will in the long term perpetuate the social discontinuity of meanings. A universalistic strategy may increase the discontinuity in the short-term by extending the level and range of conceptual endeavour but will in the long term erode the social discontinuity of meanings. Marxists would urge that in the second strategy the working class will find more for their immediate and historic purposes. Such an educational strategy comprises these elements:

(1) recognition on the part of the teacher that it is an essential part of the teacher role to stimulate conceptual development of all children;

(2) use of the classroom situation to promote peer group effort in the same direction;

(3) abandonment of selection systems within schools in favour of common learning programmes;

(4) resistance to reductions in the intellectual content of the schools' curricula.

Chapter 8

Sociology and schools

An organisational perspective

Marxists claim that their approach to social phenomena is a scientific one. They do not claim, however, that they are the only investigators attempting the development of scientific methodology in their enquiries. On the contrary, they are always ready to acknowledge and use the work of others, wherever such work can lead to clearer understanding. It is in this spirit that I take the framework of ideas provided by Martin Albrow, in the *Penguin Survey of the Social Sciences* (1965) for analysis of schools as organisations.

Especially significant in the approach is Albrow's awareness of the problem of hidden value orientations (p.148):

The problem of objectivity is endemic in social science. Crude and obvious forms of bias and wishful thinking are expunged only to be replaced by more subtle ones.

If the scientist is to reach out for objectivity he has to remember that managerial objectives in an organisation cannot exclude other objectives, that interests of different parties may not coincide, that mere declaration of value freedom is not proof of it.

'Organisational theory'—which has been applied also to schools— is criticised by Albrow because, in general, its expertise is slanted in the direction of assisting decision-making by those in power. Albrow argues that a truly sociological approach to organisations should produce theory not interested in helping the administration to achieve its goals. For example, an organisation may be defined 'as a social unit explicitly established for the achievement of specific goals', for which a division of labour, an authority structure and a set of regulations are essential. And this definition is applicable to a variety of institutions.

This definition, however, will produce bias if it is not used critically. Four major objections are raised: (i) an organisation's goals 'are not normally specific' (p.153); (ii) there is no simple congruence between organisational goals and formal procedure; (iii) group behaviour 'is not simply a function of organisational position'; (iv) 'the notion of the specific goal as the origin and cause of the organisation is an unhistorical myth'.

What is under attack is that kind of 'goal-oriented concept of organisation' whose central notion is that unless goals have a clearly understood order of importance, organisations would be unstable. But organisations maintain stability despite multiplicity of goals and conflict between them. Organisational stability therefore must depend on other factors. One of these factors, for example, may be an understanding of the mutual benefits to be derived from co-operation, so that an organisation may be seen as a 'collection of coalitions'. In such a case insistence on a clear-cut goal can result in support for one party to an agreement.

The second line of objection concerns formal procedures which are expressed in rules and regulations often limiting the pursuit of goals. Formal procedures which are taken from outside the organisation are mistakenly credited to the organisation itself and those which do arise within the organisation are mistakenly regarded as the only expression of its purposes. By implication, informal behaviours are therefore regarded as 'extrinsic helps or hindrances'. But the elements of an organisation's formal structure are its authority system and its rules and regulations. For the former a superior may require a competence not possessed by himself. That competence however (the ability of a mathematics teacher is instanced), is not bestowed by the organisation or its authority. It may be brought to or taken from the organisation. As such it is informal. 'It is not a mere help or hindrance to the authority system—it is intrinsic to its operation. The formal transmission of orders demands informal implementation' (p.157).

Rules involve the same formal-informal relationship. Only 'the agent's perception and interpretation of a situation' decide whether a rule should be applied. Such a judgment—always disputable—is informal. But despite its informality it is necessary to the working of the formal organisation. The discretion exercised is derived from the 'so-called informal elements—professional ethics, group solidarity, relations with the public, social status and many other factors'(p.158).

Besides the arguments (i) 'that the goals of organisations are not necessarily single, precise or specific' and (ii) that 'Rules may have other functions than the implementation of a "goal"' Albrow points out that members and groups may treat an organisational goal itself as being 'purely instrumental in obtaining their own purposes'(p.159). The concept of 'competing groups' and their demands is used to explain how rules governing conflict can arise within organisations.

Finally the notion of 'a common originating purpose' comes under fire. Goals and rules have long and involved histories; the founding of an organisation always involves a reorganisation of ongoing elements; how the organisation will develop is rarely foreseen; present-day complex organisations manifest a multiplicity of purposes. More important still perhaps, 'organisations may originate in the imposition of one group's purposes on another' (p.160).

In sum, we are asked to recognise, 'that organisations possess all the social characteristics of collectivities over and above their special features of goal achievement' (p.161).

The orientation suggested is that goals may be multiple, that they may have their origins outside the organisation, that they may be diffuse or precise, that they are not necessarily the initiating cause of the organisation in question. But what is especially important about organisational goals is that they legitimise the co-operative activity of their members. In parallel with Albrow's example, trade unionists say that Upper Clyde shipyards should have two main goals: the production of ships, oil rigs or other use-values embodying the special facilities and labour-power available there; the provision of a living for workers in that region. A Conservative businessman on the other hand might be more concerned with profitability. To raise profitability to the level of a 'need' and to give it priority, is to raise that legitimising principle above the other two and to enlist therefore in a power struggle.

Albrow says, 'In this situation a sociologist is not . . . to take sides'. However, once sociological analysis reveals that goal definition serves to legitimise action, and indicates other legitimising goals which may accompany or stand in opposition to profitability, is the analysis finished? There is the matter of validation. Whose writ will run? When circumstances arise in which a one-time compromise between legitimising principles becomes a conflict between them a struggle is on. The sociologist therefore has still to examine the conditions for successful validation of one principle or another, one goal or another. At this point commitment becomes an issue and Marxists cannot but commit themselves. They go beyond a classification of legitimising goals, and beyond an analysis of the struggle for priority between them: for 'The philosophers [or sociologists] have only interpreted the world differently; the point, however, is to change it'.

It is hoped that, with this addendum to the tools furnished by Albrow, insights into schools as organisations already provided will be evaluated and added to.

Goals or functions?

Royston Lambert refers to Parsons's 'pioneering work on the school class as one of the significant studies of internal constituents of the school' (1970, p.12). Parsons himself makes it clear that in his essay, 'the class, rather than the school, will be the unit of analysis because the school's essential work is done in classes' (1961, p.434). As for secondary schools, 'the complex of classes participated in by the same pupil is the significant unit' (ibid.). It becomes apparent from Parsons's account of the school class, that he is studying not merely a 'constituent part of the school' but the work of the school itself in relation to two main functions: that of training personalities 'to be motivationally and technically adequate to the performance of adult roles' and that of selection ultimately for a status in the labour force. The school's socialising processes have to be mediated by teachers in classes because as an organisation in its entirety a school cannot engage with individual pupils' role development.

We are immediately faced then with a choice of concepts: is it better to regard schools and their classes as having 'functions', or as collectivities wherein various goals are pursued? Whilst goals are not even mentioned in Parsons's essay there is certainly an abundance of major and minor functions. The children are thought of as units in various stages of preparation for fitness to perform complicated and multifaceted acts. But the acts are well known and are predetermined. They are working 'mechanisms' of a plant whose peculiarity is that it reproduces, unceasingly, its own working parts. The plant is society. The mechanisms are statuses. In motion the statuses are roles.

Now we have taken the view that roles in the form of identities personify the 'shared learned meanings' of a society. As such they must regenerate presently the outcome of its cultural past. But the 'actors' in their roles are not script-bound. They not only derive prescribed purposes from their situtations, they create new purposes. Engels recognised this and he showed that since the actualities resulting from goal seeking do not coincide with the intentions, these social actualities may be investigated like any others (1958, edn p.253).

the conflict of innumerable wills and individual actions in the domain of history produce a state of affairs entirely analogous to that prevailing in the realm of unconscious nature. The ends of the actions are intended, but the results which actually follow from these actions are not intended; or when they do seem to correspond to the end intended, they ultimately have consequences quite other than those intended.

Whereas Parsons makes children's and teachers' activities (like those of people generally speaking) functional mechanisms in a social system, Engels systematises history from the succession of events that result from the intentions of human beings.

For Parsons one problem is 'how the school class functions to internalise in its pupils . . . commitment and capacities for successful performance of their future adult roles . . . and . . . to allocate these human resources within the role structure of adult society' (1961, p.434). The school class is an agency, in concert with family, peer groups and other agencies, for carrying out these functions. Here Parsons closely follows Durkheim's ideas in breaking up commitment into (i) the broad values of society, or conformity to expectations of interpersonal behaviour and (ii) a specific type of role and capacity, or competence to perform individually in an occupation.

Another problem is how, as an agency of manpower allocation, the American elementary school, succeeded by junior high school, functions most crucially in determining who 'do and do not go to college'.

When Parsons discusses selection and the bearing that social class has upon this process he is at pains to prove that selection is 'genuinely assortive' (ibid., p.436). He admits that fathers' occupations are easily detectable in the allocations. But he explains this is a consequence of the ascriptive factors having some influence on achievement factors. He insists that the 'essential' point is 'a relatively uniform criterion of selection'. That criterion is 'a single main axis of achievement'.

For identification of achievers the school class structure has four primary features: initial equality of contestants; a common set of tasks; one teacher representative of the adult world; and systematic evaluation of pupils' performances. In line again with Durkheim's views on pedagogical functions, Parsons states that the content of achievement is of two types: cognitive learning including acquisiton of skills, facts, the beginning of literacy and numeracy; moral learning including acceptable attitudes to teacher, to fellow-pupils, to work and capacities for 'leadership' and 'initiative'. The importance of this for the school, according to Parsons, is that it is 'broadly' functional for selective process. Teacher is an adult. Achievement-motivation is learnt by identification with teacher. However, identification may take place with the peer group instead. These alternatives in identification match the split into college-goers and non-college-goers respectively and 'in the school system is the primary source of selective dichotomization' (p.443).

The role of the teacher is also primarily related to the function of selection. She is, like parents, an adult, but her role is a universalistic one and it is bound up with children's performances and their order of achievement. 'Above all she must be the agent of bringing about and legitimising a differentiation of the school class on an achievement axis' (p.444).

From the foregoing summary of Parsons's analysis, it should be clear that not only does this go beyond an examination of the elementary school class to an account of the school's work as a whole, but it also contains the main lines of description of educational institutions in general. Indeed his final word on the exercise is, 'I think it has been possible to sketch out a few of the major structural patterns of the public [state] school system' (p.453).

Now the views of Parsons though clearly labelled 'American' are not unacceptable in England. A few modifications would have to be introduced to make the system more 'British'. But anyone familiar with primary and secondary education in this country will recognise the processes in our schools and may easily fall prone to accept this functional view of education.

The starting point of the criticism is to suggest that there is an affinity between the unitary, clear-cut, commonly-held-goal understanding of organisations and the view outlined, in that both have a built-in value orientation supporting one set of class interests. But the function definition is more effective in giving this support. For what this does is to call the practice serving certain purposes a function. And in doing so the vital interests inherent in those purposes, the identities of their creators and executors and the social class intentions behind them are effectively hidden. When a sociologist talks about goals, anyone may ask, 'Whose goals?'. But if he talks about functions then responsibility for policy, for direction, for educational method, for declared aims of education appears as an irrelevance.

The practice of accurate streaming or of valid indication of position-in-class can be seen as a goal. But their very perception as goals may lead to identification of the persons and groups creating and pursuing them. Goals, moreover, may be compared one with another, may even be regarded as obsolete, or not worth pursuit. That is to say, legitimation has to be established where goals are concerned.

In Parsons's usage the 'mechanism' and the 'function' have no authors. Mechanism and function are governing factors. As such they are not subject to legitimation. They even serve as grounds of legitimation. But if we think about it, there is no single named 'function' in Parsons's account—selection, socialisation, training, internalisation of commitment, internalisation of capacity, allocation of human resources, determination of who goes to college—that may not be called a goal.

It becomes clear therefore that what is accomplished theoretically by thinking in terms of function instead of goals is evasion of the legitimising argument. And the practical outcome is consolidation of those incumbents of power pursuing their own interests in the education system as a whole—pursuing their own goals.

This is not to say that 'function' has no place in discussions concerning schools. Parents with children in primary schools may imbue them with a drive towards grammar school, or grammar stream in the comprehensive school and encourage them to achieve that goal. Whatever is done in the junior school class is judged then in terms of function. That is, a parent's key question is likely to be, 'How well does this class prepare my child for selection for a highly valued kind of secondary education?'

Function here becomes the means and process whereby goals are striven for. A teacher, however, does not necessarily accept such a function as being a major characteristic of his role. It is not at all unlikely that a teacher will regard intra-class differentiation on an achievement scale as something altogether undesirable. His objectives may well be such goals as the beginning of a love of music in children, the stimulation in children of creative expression in writing and in painting, the enjoyment of childhood as a phase of life in its own right with its own types of fulfilment. And the more successful a teacher is in these kinds of achievement the more role-performance satisfaction will he experience. In this case, goals of the parents, who send their children to school with occupational objectives in view, become functional for the goals of the teacher. So, one man's goals are another man's functions. None the less, in the view of either party, the function is subordinate to the goal.

Given a system of education which, in a competitive society, is fundamentally competitive, what one child learns will eventually be measured against what another child learns. Given the autonomy of the school (and considerable autonomy of the teachers in the school class) education may sponsor co-operation. Teachers will not refuse to teach on account of the first factor, nor will parents withhold their children from school on account of the second factor. In practice, what emerges is a combination of goals each of which makes the other possible—each of which is functional for the other. But the inherent contradiction between the goals is not thereby eradicated.

On such a view the examination of schools in terms of goals will be more satisfactory than their examination in terms of function.

In addition to what may be called 'functional apology' there is other evidence that functional analysis of the school conceals support for purposes imposed upon it. One is Parsons's reluctance to analyse educational practice of a sort other than selection, in respect of its relation to the social structure as a whole. The important 'qualification', the progressive school with emphasis on projects, on co-operation, on permissiveness, on group work, and 'de-emphasis on formal marking' (1961, p.438) is associated with the mode of 'early socialisation in the family' (ibid.). As he says, 'the relation of support for progressive education to relatively high economic status . . . is well-known' (ibid.), one might expect some analysis of the relation between non-selecting socialising educational agencies and its 'function' from a 'societal point of view'. This, however, is not gone into.

More revealing is Parsons's proof that selection is 'genuinely assortative' (p.436). The advantage of better-off families' children over those of poorer families is imputed to 'ascriptive factors' though these do, admittedly, influence achievement. What this means is that children of parents with high socio-economic status have a better chance at school. What makes everything fair—the 'essential' thing— is that the advantaged and the disadvantaged are subject to a 'uniform criterion of selection'!

Now ascription is a term we have used to identify a process of role acquisition. If socio-economic status is an ascriptive factor then the modes of socialisation and its agencies will be such as to create a high expectation from the children of all social classes that they will acquire roles corresponding to their social status of origin. That of course is what broadly happens and the impartiality of selection criteria ensures that it does happen. That this is so is shown by Parsons's figures to the effect that 70 per cent of children of labourers in the top quintile of ability were not intended by their parents to try for college as against 11 per cent of similar children of major white collar workers.

The so-called 'initial equality of the contestants' is shown also to be an inequality. It is just in passing that the assertion is made that the initial equality is guaranteed by the homogeneity of the elementary school class. The elementary school is a neighbourhood school and neighbourhoods are generally homogeneous in respect of social class. Thus advantages accruing from socio-economic status—'the neighbourhood being typically more homogeneous than is the whole society' (ibid., p.438)—are not given effect in the school class. The difference between elementary schools is not remarked upon, presumably because this is just one more ascriptive factor. As we know from the Plowden Report, the difference between schools at the primary stage is one of the major sources of initial inequality—at any rate in English education. And one gathers from Margaret Mead's article, 'The school in American culture' (Halsey, Floud and Anderson, 1961) that this is true for the USA also.

The public school model

The fruitfulness of organisational analysis with goal definition as its keystone is shown in the work of Royston Lambert. His model is outlined in his introduction to *The Public Schools* (1966) by Kalton and becomes a lens through which we are enabled to see the major characteristics of the public school and how these stand in contrast with those of state schools.

The links between the goals of the public schools as defined by them and those goals derived from forces beyond them are not forged in, but 'immediate external factors' are clearly set out: independence of public authority; selective intake; service to the 'upper income groups'; government and staffing from within the same system; careful preparation for admission; high coincidence between values and expectations of parents and pupils on the one side and of the school on the other. Besides these factors there are: the scope of the school's influence over succeeding generations of some of its families, over the preparatory schools, universities, friendship groups and occupation groups. 'In short, the public school is an integral part of a whole sub-system of our society: exclusive, self-contained, with a common value system, partly self perpetuating, but not closed or static' (p.xiv). The ambiguity here—whether the terms that follow the colon qualify the school or the subsystem—is a helpful one. It shows that they define both what Marxists call 'the ruling class' and its specialised educational institutions and also that the qualities of the class are guaranteed by the qualities of the school. And we shall see that if the public school is not a completely 'closed' or 'total' institution, the openings are narrow and well-guarded.

The main elements in Lambert's model are four: goals, formal structure, informal system, cultural and value system goals of the school are classified. The pursuit of instrumental goals is engaged in by the acquisition of skill and knowledge for use as 'means to ends'. Expressive goals are ends in themselves—character building, sensitivity orientation, and gratification of immediate needs. Implementation of organisational goals ensures continuance and well-being of the school as such. Range and weighting attached to these goals may differ from one type of school to another. As is pointed out, the boarding public school pursues a far wider range of expressive aims than the state schools can manage and its various pressures for loyalty to the school can be stronger and more effective (p.xv):

> unlike their counterparts in state schools public school boys are kept more consciously aware of the school's aims as a whole: they are constantly being stressed for example in sermons, in speeches, in literature and symbolised in tradition and rituals.

Formal organisation is expressed in a series of administrations for academic work, cultural and recreational activities and pastoral care of the pupils. Besides being more complex than in state schools formal organisation administers the pursuit of different instrumental goals. Technical, manual and commercial subjects are largely excluded from public school curricula which favour academic learning. Thorough and continuous supervision involves pupils as well as staff and gives rise to an elaboration and sophistication not to be found in state schools.

The roles and statuses in such a complex formal organisation are also largely exclusive and inward looking. Staff role-sets are built on expectations of their playing a series of roles in different departments with a 'high and diffuse level of commitment' (p.xviii). This contrasts with more circumscribed commitment of teachers in state schools in terms of time and diversity of role.

Pupils' roles in public schools are more school-based than in state schools. This dispossesses the former of home-based and neighbour-hood-based roles. In the course of time pupils 'assume roles similar to those expected of the staff or adults more frequently than in the state school' (ibid.). Membership of a near-total institution is consolidated by a process in which pupils' time is deliberately planned to demand continuous attention to school tasks and aims. Contact with the outside society is thus strictly regulated and alienation from society in general is enforced.

Authority is defined by Lambert as 'power which is accepted as legitimate' (p.xxii). Its hierarchical distribution among staff and pupils is derived from office held in the house and school teams and so on. Exercise of authority as well as obedience will be experienced by every pupil, thus linking informal power systems with formally organised authority. This contrasts with state schools where formal authority may not be possessed by pupils no matter what real influence they have.

Formal control over contact with the outside world limits public schools to association 'mainly with schools of similar kind, status and social composition' (p.xxiv) and maintains its authoritarian, totalitarian insularity.

Informal interactions vary in their relations with formal groupings. The range in public schools runs 'from co-operation or manipulation at one extreme through awareness to suppression at the other' (p.xxv). But the characteristic is to 'manipulate or embrace the informal society', so that the end result is support for the goals of the formal organisation. In state schools on the other hand, outside role systems make them less controllable. Pupils' informal organisations are therefore 'suppressed, just recognised or ignored'.

At this point Lambert introduces Merton's range of possible reactions on the part of pupils to their perception of the goals formally pursued by the schools. They may rebel (set up their own goals against them); retreat (reject them); conform; accept method but not ultimate ends (ritualists); accept ends but seek to alter methods (innovators). Rebellion and retreatism are held to be more common in state schools but more extreme in public schools—for, 'the more total an institution, the more extreme will be the modes of adaptation to it' (p.xxvii).

Two other contrasts are made. In public schools pupils and staff relate to each other both formally and informally; in state schools the informal pressures from both sides insist upon formality as the mode of staff-pupil interaction. More fundamental however, is the fact that public schools share values not only with each other but also with 'the wider social system of which they are a part and whose values they reflect and shape'. This contrasts with the variety of value orientations to be found both within and between state schools.

The superiority of this goal-centred model for the analysis of schools over one centred on function is quite apparent. Here is a tool which leads to the discovery of purposes at work and which, as a consequence, facilitates the comparison of types of school, one with another. The definition of goals, the analysis of formal and informal organisation working towards them and the description of avenues of contact with the outside society prohibit hidden, gross support of concealed but none the less real aims and intentions.

Even this analysis, however, cannot be left without pointing to certain alterations, additions and conclusions which must be made if a Marxist perspective is to be drawn. To begin with there is the compliance on Lambert's part with the unwritten and unstated law, observed by nearly all—if not all—writers on the sociology of education, that the capitalist class must not be referred to as such. Whilst the print will occasionally dare the word 'capitalism', by tacit agreement the term 'capitalist class' is censored. Instead 'middle class', or 'upper class' or 'upper income groups' or 'subsystems of our society'—appellations which do not immediately reveal the exploitative relationship with the rest of society are brought into use. And it must be said that this ritual is itself functional to the self-preservation ends of the capitalist class even when its practitioners intend merely to use conventional terminology.

For the public schools are pre-eminently that system of institutions especially fostered within capitalist society to preserve, develop and, strengthen the class consciousness and class solidarity of succeeding generations of the capitalist class and their recuits. It is the intention of individual capitalists that their sons especially shall be socialised in such a way as to become successful capitalists themselves. It is the goal of organisations of capitalists—businesses, political parties, clubs and so on—to sustain and to create conditions in which the activities of capitalists can flourish: and one of these conditions is the network of public schools. It is the central aim of the leaders of the capitalist class that capitalism as a system of society shall endure, and for this it is crucial that the socialisation processes for each succeeding generation shall be expertly brought to bear in order that the appropriate norms and values should be internalised. The public schools and their preparatory schools are a highly sophisticated machinery for achieving this end.

For the working class there exists no comparable means for the fostering in its succeeding generations of such a class consciousness and solidarity. Nor within capitalism can such a machinery come into being. For the preconditions of such a school system are the possession of economic and political power. What is possible, however, is the pursuit of a strategy in respect of school provision which (i) augments the strength of the working class in the struggle it carries on against exploitation, and (ii) promises to become, in embryo, the school system of the future. Moreover, the content of such class consciousness must—above all in education—carry reference to the socialism which only the working class can inaugurate. This class consciousness includes the awareness that class society must give way, under working-class rule, to classless society, the view that internationalism must supersede chauvinism, the ethic that concepts of humanity must overtake concepts of racism and imperialism.

In short the pursuit of social consciousness and social solidarity is what must characterise the goals of schools when and where power falls to the hands of a victorious proletariat. It matters very much therefore what kinds of school structure, and what kinds of educational administration are left by capitalism for adaptation to the purposes of the builders of the new order.

What has here been added to Lambert's model is an element suggested in this chapter's first remarks on goals of complex organisations. Goals must have sources and seekers. They are striven after by persons and groups of persons, and unless the interests of these groups and persons are isolated and named the goals appear as if in a disembodied manifestation. As a consequence their meanings cannot be properly understood. Since the goal sources may be external to the school they should be classified as such and labelled to differentiate them from goals specific to the school.

The model discussed has been built upon considerably. Its more elaborate development is in Lambert, Bullock and Millham's, *A Manual to the Sociology of the School*. Here are to be found formulations which almost grasp principles which might orient school-given-goals to the struggle between the major classes in capitalist society. But here too is to be found the major conceptual barrier to such a grasp.

To discover the barrier to the viewpoint favoured here it is necessary to go to the preface of the *Manual*. For it is here that the history of school-as-an-organisation analysis is outlined. This was in the first place seen 'as an agency of allocation . . . of social mobility' (1970, p.11). The contribution of sociologists working in the field of education was its help in reducing 'the influence of social class differences on schools as allocative systems and thus to extend opportunities of education and social mobility' (p.12). Side by side with this grew studies of schools' internal dynamics. The specifically new contribution which the *Manual* claims to herald is 'a theory or empirical framework by which the school can be understood and explored as a coherent and distinct social organisation in its own right' (ibid.).

What is intended is the prosecution of a line of enquiry which will not emphasise the sorting-out functions prescribed for schools. Instead the emphasis will fall upon 'the school's function as an *integrative* mechanism for society . . . and of the transmission of the culture of society, its values, norms and their accepted modes of expression and renewal' (ibid.).

Such an approach will be familiar to those who know Durkheim's

Education and Sociology where the exhortation is repeatedly made for attention to the dual function of schools: that of being sensitive to the social division of labour; that of inculcating the morality of the society as a whole.

For goal-oriented sociologists there is some difficulty in following Durkheim. For, in spite of his insistence that action is always constrained, Durkheim lectured his student pedagogues as though there would be from pupils and from others, no constantly renewed, vital and forceful pursuit of ends not in harmony with those proposed for them. Yet, conflict is the fact, recognised not alone by socio-logical enquiry but also by many practising teachers who reject selection as a central purpose of their work and who find difficulty in accepting the overall values of capitalist society. Thus those who attempt to understand schools find themselves compelled to examine those forces, inside and outside schools, which express and sustain goals other than and opposed to either selection or legitimation of capitalism—or both.

These forces, whether represented by pupil behaviour, by trade union resolution, by unceasing action at local and national level, in articles and essays, or in more elaborate statements, are, more or less strongly linked with the working class.

Now there are, and must be, goals generated by the schools as such—that is, goals specific to the school. By way of an analogy, given a capitalist economy responding only to market forces, house-building is started in order to make interest and profit. The rate of house-building will fluctuate in accordance with rates of return on the capital invested in that activity as compared with rates of return elsewhere. Knowledge of the economics of house-building, however, will teach no one to lay bricks, to be a carpenter or a plumber, or the elements of house design. As Marx indicated, the corporate labour-power used by the capitalists to bring him surplus value has many other attributes. Not the least of these is a growing consciousness that the capitalist is himself surplus to social need. And so it must be with education. Education is not fully understood when the capi-talist interest therein is identified. Schools are organisations of social endeavour which, though they take their form and many of their goals from capitalist relationships, have other goals besides, goals which may transcend and even oppose these relationships. That social endeavour is engaged in most directly by the pupils and the teachers who are in the schools.

Consensus and conflict in schools

To an important degree, but without the class definition, an important contribution to such an understanding of schools is made in M. D. Shipman's *Sociology of the School* (1968). Here the fullest use is made of a wide range of sociological concepts and of empirical investigation to make us aware of the forces at work within the schools.

It will be recognised that many of the criticisms made of other writings on the sociology of education are applicable also to Shipman's: there is no recognition of capitalism and of class purposes; the unhistoric myth of a definite aim for which the school was organised is set forth as a gospel; selection and allocation, purposes which serve the capitalist class, are shown to be ineluctable functions which must be fulfilled; other, minor, sources of classroom conflict are bracketed with awareness of educational deprivation and are given equal weight with it.

One other criticism may be advanced. Shipman's justifiable readiness to use a variety of theoretical tools of analysis appears to have resulted in a disinclination to discriminate between them. In consequence, several contradictions emerge in the work. But these contradictions are as much the outcome of the unfitness of certain of the theories for living reality as of anything else. The notion that rewards in schools are 'essentially symbolic . . . building up [a pupil's] commitment' (1968, p.102) cannot live easily at the side of the assertion that 'all teachers in all schools' allocate and select for different occupational statuses. Neither can the latter pronouncement fit the illustration given 'of a large junior school which abandoned streaming' (pp.158–9). Similarly, it is difficult to reconcile the idea that 'the cultural goals served by the schools determine not only their internal organisation but also their external relations' (p.49) with the idea that the work of preparing children 'for positions in adult life . . . largely determines the organisation of schools'.

Difficulties like these are bound to arise when on the one hand the study of schools is anchored firmly in the schools themselves and on the other hand the theoretical tools of analysis are as firmly anchored to the purposes of a ruling class as we have shown the Sorokin and the Parsons models to be. Indeed, the schools themselves represent the very contradictions which seem logically incompatible.

How does this situation come about? The process is particularly discernible to those of us whose special work it is to prepare intending teachers for their profession. The student on 'teaching practice' has to equip himself with attitude, knowledge and method for interaction in an ideal way with a group of children. This involves: (i) getting to know the pupils and their abilities; (ii) selecting what, from the store of human knowledge, skill and criteria, they ought next to try to master; (iii) deciding upon a method of presentation suitable to the matter and to the children; (iv) anticipating strains and difficulties that may be encountered in the course of 'the scheme of work' or of the 'lesson' and developing strategies to meet them. In other words the essential nexus between teacher and pupil is what Shipman calls the 'transmission' of knowledge, values, skill and the wakening of sensitivity and awareness. Fulfilment for the teacher comes from his knowledge that the pupils have made a positive response to his efforts. Pupil satisfaction comes from their experience of a growing mastery of the mysteries of their world.

But this is the educational situation. A sustained repetition of such situations throughout a school year creates a continuous tendency on the part of schools to generate educational goals, to produce, that is to say, complementary teacher-pupil interaction around problems of learning. The conditions of learning thus become a major concern for the teacher whose position in this interaction with his pupils induces in him the need to evolve the expertise required for his role.

It should be remarked that the 'rewards' available from successful teaching-learning are to be obtained from the process itself, just as the arrival at a solution affords the major satisfaction in any problem-solving activity. In this sense all learning associated with so-called 'instrumental goals' are expressive—just as it can be shown that, in another sense, all the activity associated with 'expressive goals' are instrumental. There is joy in learning and there is learning in joy.

But the socialisation process inherent in the educational situation is accompanied by and interwoven with others. To become an adult in a capitalist society does mean, for any working-class son or daughter, taking a position in the occupational hierarchy. Since the state schools are the schools provided by the capitalist state, that is, by the power-wielding apparatus of the capitalist class, it is found convenient to press from the very beginning for the implementation of its goals. These goals include preparation of children for their positions as adult workers. Accordingly, there have had to be 'codes' for schools, or 'suggestions for teachers' or a body of psychometric evidence to show that certain children cannot profit from attempting to learn a foreign language, or algebra, or follow a worthwhile science course. And anyway, what would be the point in view of the ultimate job to be filled? In this way schools are given tasks and teachers are assigned roles which are not germane to the educational situation. To fulfil the goals defined for schools by the capitalist class, there must be—not a continuous assessment of what children have accomplished so that new horizons may be brought into view, but selection, position in class, promotions and demotions from one stream to another, successes and failures in the race for these positions. Accompanying the whole process are the maintenance of rigour and high expectation in the 'A' stream and the emptying of syllabuses, with correspondingly lower expectation in the lower streams.

On this view teachers mediate or are agents of cultural forces in two ways. They bring to school with their own education a fund of society's accumulated knowledge. They act also, on behalf of children's future employers, as agents of selection and allocation. But they do more. They create, sustain and develop the educational institutions in which they work. The consequent demands which must be made upon society by the schools ultimately depend upon teachers' endeavour. Indeed theirs is a vital and growing part in the definition, constantly revised, of what society generally must do for education. In this continuous redefinition teachers express, not only their own needs but those of their pupils and, in a special way, the aspirations of parents.

It is in this sense that Shipman's intrinsic argument is correct: schools have, to a degree, their own dynamic. One hesitates to call it a culture for the reason that, as they are analysed here, schools are institutions where the bearers of subcultures meet the cultural heritage of society as a whole. But the fact that schools generate their own impulse to the form and content of social continuity calls for a revision of the widespread formula that schools are agencies, only, for the transmission of culture. We need to think of them as organisations which constitute an intrinsic part of society, a major element in its structure, a vital branch of its culture.

As Shipman shows, the selection process imposed upon schools does not always harmonise with the educational process. The conflict which arises from the disharmony is expressed, however, beyond the classroom, beyond the school, in administrative machinery, in teachers' professional associations and in politics. How this conflict is likely to be resolved depends on society's order of values: education first or selection?

At this point class interest is manifest. For the capitalist class the important function of the schools is to provide employees with various levels of accomplishment. But the proletariat as a class—that is, through its spokesmen and its representative institutions—asserts that it is education which matters. There is therefore a sound basis for the suggestion that teachers' goals coincide with those of the working class unless they are themselves drawn into the race for selection. It would seem that there is a strong trend in favour of education with a consequently greater readiness on the part of teachers' organisations to ally themselves with other working-class forces.

Selection has in this conflict the power of the state in its favour. This power bears, currently, the face of authority. That is, it is legitimated—held generally to be just. But as John Rex remarks in *New Society* (6 October, 1972), 'such authority rests, as we all know from our experience, on a solid basis of apathy, rather than on any feeling that it is truly legitimate'. Besides apathy there is a reward system for teachers to engage as agents of selection in the allocative machinery so that teachers are moved to do their delegated authority roles. The 'them against us' understanding of some pupils is thus, in part, a matter of accurate perception in many cases. But this is balanced by its negation when pupils experience the satisfaction of learning.

Enough has been said here to show why it is that for Marxists the development of knowledge concerning the conditions of learning is of considerable importance as a facet of class struggle.

Although P. W. Musgrave (1968a) defines an organisation as a 'system of co-ordinated activity carried out by two or more persons for a definite purpose', his starting point for discussing 'schools as organisations' is to define four goal areas each one of which has a history. One of these areas is religion, another, élitism in rivalry with egalitarianism, a third, economic and a fourth is independence.

Musgrave does not discuss why it was that the various groups who in the first place pressed for secular education, came to an understanding which perpetuated denomination schools and ensured the teaching of religion in all state schools. But there is no mystery about this. This is something not at all unusual in the armoury of bourgeois

control. Marx, in *The Eighteenth Brumaire of Napoleon Bonaparte*
writes of the events in France following the June defeat of the
proletariat in Paris in 1848 (1969 edn., p.370):

> Never did the bourgeoisie rule more absolutely. Never did it
> display more ostentatiously the insignia of domination.
>
> I have not here to write the history of its legislative activity,
> which is summarised during this period in two laws: in the law
> re-establishing the *wine tax*, and the *education law* abolishing
> unbelief.

Engels in an essay *On Historical Materialism*, after recapitulating
the revolutionary upsurge in Europe from 1848 to 1851 writes (1969
edn., pp.102–3):

> For a time at least the bugbear of working-class pretensions was
> put down, but at what cost! If the British bourgeois had been
> convinced before of the necessity of maintaining the common
> people in a religious mood, how much more must he feel the
> necessity after all these experiences? Regardless of the sneers of
> his Continental compeers, he continued to spend thousands and
> tens of thousands, year after year, upon the evangelisation of
> the lower orders.

And in the same essay on the situation in England after 1867 (p.106)

> Now, if ever, the people must be kept in order by moral means,
> and the first and foremost of all moral means of action upon
> the masses is and remains—religion. Hence the parsons'
> majorities on the school boards, hence the increasing self-
> taxation of the bourgeoisie for the support of all kinds of
> revivalism, from ritualism to the Salvation Army.

To return to Musgrave and his second goal area. Here the pursuit
by the social classes of their different goals in the creation of appropriate schools and curricula is recognisable. Clarity is reduced
however by the now familiar reluctance to name social classes
appropriately. (There has been no capitalist class, no land-owning
class.) 'Élite' and 'élitism' is substituted for ruling class and claim to
class privilege. There is also the loose way in which the term 'political
power' is used. That the capitalist class was in effective political
control after 1832 is a fact. But the term 'middle class' seems to
express a notion that includes both capitalist and professional, and
leads to the proposition that 'the middle class came nearer to
political power' (1968, p.13).

The ground is thus prepared for the assertion that 'the second reform of parliament in 1867 in its turn allowed the working class to approach political power' (p.14). But at this time no working-class political party has taken shape, the rebirth of the trade union movement has but just begun and the conquest of political power was an aim of none of the new craft unions typical of that and the following decade.

Area three, that concerned with economic goals, includes require-ments from schools on the part of dominant groups in industry and commerce, who influence curricula and the definition of goals by headmasters and teachers. But for some reason at this point there is a switch from analysis in terms of goals to one in terms of function (p.18):

> By the mid-twentieth century the social function of education
> especially vis-à-vis the economy has come to be paramount . . . .
> In brief, the needs of the economy have influenced the scale and
> nature of educational provision.

We have already made the point that the transformation of policies of more or less powerful groups, into anonymous social processes of 'function', 'needs of the economy' and so on in effect hides very real identities.

Concerning independence Musgrave points out that it 'remains a strong tradition in British education, and this goal carries the rider that the first three must somehow be thoroughly instilled in teachers and administrators' (p.21). Teachers then must support religion, pay lip-service to equality but practice élitism by making sure that their teaching subserves the labour requirements of the economy. On such a view no aims for education stem directly from educational practice, but this does not altogether accord with the facts of life.

Now Marxists understand full well that for a society to subsist large areas of expectation must be beyond question, that institutions must 'function' for each other in fulfilment of each other's goals. They also understand that there must be institutions which enable this fulfilment to be realised. The importance they attach to class antagonism however—in the modern age the struggle between the bourgeoisie and the proletariat—brings them to appreciate that stability is ensured by a highly complex state power. Political power, during a period of stability, is generally the power of the class with social power—with dominance valid throughout the weave of the social fabric: that is, in this country, at this time, of the capitalist class. As for the government, the government is itself the leading committee of the state apparatus, of the political power. The government would cease to be this if it moved to challenge the social power; it could cease to be this only at a time when the working class sought power for itself as a class. Labour governments have been acceptable to the capitalist class because they have challenged neither its social nor its political power.

This understanding by Marxists, of the nature of state power, of government and of their special relevance to the issues of class struggle, leads them to reject 'general will' theories such as that expressed by Musgrave (p.23):

Once the members of a society have come to an agreement,
whether by conscious process or merely through unconscious
acceptance, on the goals for education, a more or less exact
definition becomes possible of the way in which these goals will
be translated into administrative machinery.

Instead, Marxists enjoin the critical study of Acts, Regulations, analyses, and recommendations from whatever quarter, with the interests of the contending groups kept in mind as the motivations of intentions enshrined therein. To look upon an Education—or any other—Act as an outcome of agreement between citizens all with equal standing, equal influence and equal access to information is, admittedly, widespread. This last fact does not make the standpoint any less erroneous, nor does it make its exponents any the less responsible for the perpetuation of the error.

We return to Albrow's proposition which indicates that the sociologist's task is to find the multiple goals and the identities of their pursuants both within and outside the formal organisations (schools, administrative bodies, departments) and we return to our own extension of that view—an extension which commits the investigator to the support of working-class interests.

An application of Marxist method

No mode of investigation can meet these requirements better than the Marxist method which holds that social phenomena must be studied historically—that is as events in motion, that particular social phenomena can only be understood in relation to the whole society, that the force behind the dynamic of events is ultimately the technology at man's disposal, and that the dynamic itself in class society is the struggle between antagonistic classes. This is the method employed in Brian Simon's *Education and the Labour Movement* (1965), a book especially relevant to a discussion on schools because certain types of school as they arose in England, are discussed in terms of their socio-historical context and the class goals they encompassed.

Thus in regard to public schools, the social pressures of a dominant capitalist class after 1832 gave rise to proprietary schools in 1840. The bourgeois demand for educational privilege is shown to inspire headmasters and governors to shake off local responsibilities and to transform endowed grammar schools into schools for the rich.

Against that, the story is traced of working-class aims in education epitomised in Smyth's evidence to the Cross Commission on Elementary Education (1887). Smyth, a plasterer, represented the London Trades Council and wanted 'all the roads to education open, free and unfettered to the people right up to university level'. Moreover he wanted the school to be non-vocational but 'to give a general education . . . in one school "common to all" ' (Simon's summary, 1965, pp.122–6).

The political aims of an imperialist ruling class and their necessary complements in public schools and in a second tier of privileged schools are fully documented. And so is the deliberate drive for their implementation by Balfour, Gorst and Robert Morant.

But it is the reality of the growth of goals specific to the school which is of great interest to us here. The board schools, inaugurated by the 1870 Act to fill the gaps left by church schools, had consequences not foreseen by their founders. From the interaction of teachers with pupils in these schools there were generated new ways of coping with their cultural heritage. If then they grew in popularity and extended their curricula, if increasing numbers stayed on to thirteen, fourteen and even fifteen, if they used certain grants to facilitate this development into a new type of secondary education in 'higher grade schools' this was not at all to the liking of the ruling class. On the one hand A. P. Laurie, Assistant Commissioner to the Bryce Commission (1895) could say 'This higher grade school represents a new educational movement from below and a demand from new classes of the population for Secondary Education which has sprung up in a few years' (quoted in Simon, 1965, p.179). On the other hand a Conservative government elected in 1895 found it necessary to mount a vigorous attack upon them.

The Cockerton judgment was a victory for the ruling class. But the bitter struggle that preceded the passing of the 1902 Act found the working class—especially the Trades Union Congress—in opposition to Morant and making its own definition of working-class educational objectives. These included no legitimation of a selection system (quoted in ibid., p.202):

> The system of providing secondary education only for a small proportion of workers' children who can come to the top after severe competition with their school fellows is strongly to be condemned.

To this opposition, and to such a definition, broadly in support of the higher grade schools, the National Union of Teachers lent its strength.

All educational aims—sometimes more, sometimes less clearly formulated—of the working class have revolved around its central demand for secondary education for all. This has had two aspects: raising the school leaving age, and the creation of a non-competitive secondary school system which would be end-on to primary education. These goals have had to meet the changing needs of capitalist production and the insistence of the capitalist class that any form of education for working-class children must be restricted in scope and must have occupational-selection functions. As F. Clarke wrote in *Freedom in the Educative Society* (1948, pp.122–6).

> True, such of the dominant culture as was thought necessary for them (the town workers) was conceded in the form of elementary education. But the early history of elementary education in England abounds in illustrations of the grudging nature of that concession and of the intention to restrict it to the narrowest possible limits. More important still is the fact that what was conceded was that share in accepted culture which, in nature and amount, was considered necessary in the interests, not of those who received it, but of those who granted it.

But if the major struggle between the two antagonistic classes has been expressed in conflicts there have been its compromises too.

In the complexity of conflict and compromise, gains for the labour movement were, after the First World War, the end of half-time exemptions (Education Act 1918) and the consequent compulsory schooling up to fourteen with a promise that it would be increased by a year, and the beginnings of post-primary education at the end of the twenties. Selection was to remain, however, and it was reinforced by the formula 'selection by differentiation'. This was carried forward in a system of secondary education with four kinds of establishment: grammar schools, central selective schools, central schools, and senior classes. But differentiation of children one from another was begun early in primary schools based on the expectation of ultimate placing. By 1938 an ideological legitimation for the structure had appeared in the form of psychometric theory. From the Spens Report then came the recommendations for the tripartite organisation of secondary education in grammar, technical and modern schools.

What opposition there was to selection between the wars was weak. Even when concessions could be forced by a politically strong working class during and after the Second World War, there was no opposition to selection. Yet the 1944 Act bore no reference to different sorts of secondary school, so that when the movement began during the later 1940s to press for comprehensive schools there was no legal impediment to this. From 1951 to 1964 even Conservative governments made concessions to comprehensive secondary schools. What made all the difference was the accumulation of changes in the labour requirements of the economy: unskilled workers were in diminishing demand at one extreme, professionals were in increasing demand at the other.

The requirement for a more highly educated labour force, the raising of the school leaving age to fifteen, and the faith of secondary modern school teachers in their pupils left only one more barrier to a change in the nature of these schools. Thus, once the General Certificate of Education took the place of the School Certificate (1951), and the minimum age of eligibility was lowered to fifteen (1953), new possibilities opened up for the secondary moderns. 'By 1954, a year after lowering the age of entry, over 5,000 pupils from modern schools up and down the country were entered [for examination]; by the summer of 1962 the figure had soared to 37,000' (Rubinstein and Simon, 1969, p.56).

We should emphasise here that industrial requirements have lately made reorganisation of secondary education a goal to be pursued— not consistently and always with reservations—by capitalist interests. On the other hand the century from 1870 to 1970 has witnessed a deliberate, persistent struggle of the working-class movement to achieve the 'common school' and secondary education for all. That struggle is not at an end, but in the comprehensive schools the movement against all forms of segregation has a stronger base than ever it had.

Comprehensives and class struggle

So determined has been the pressure for the establishment of the comprehensive school, and over so long a time, that it would be a serious deficiency here to omit reference to Julienne Ford's search for an answer to the pertinent question: are the hopes invested in the reorganisation of secondary education being realised in practice?

In *Social Class and the Comprehensive School* (1969) seven propositions are taken together as constituting the theory inspiring the policy responsible for its creation. These propositions involve criticism of the tripartite system and claims for the comprehensive alternative.

Ford tests four of these propositions by comparisons of what actually happens in (i) a grammar school; (ii) a secondary modern school; and (iii) a comprehensive school. The propositions not tested are the first concerning the frustration of talent with the reversal of this tendency given a comprehensive system, and the last concerning early selection. The outcome of the research is that 'comprehensive education as it is practised at present' (p.41) does not change the characteristic association between social class and education attainment, will not 'result in a widening of occupational horizons' (p.66), will not reduce class bias in informal social relations within the classroom and will not reduce class consciousness. A chapter on the first proposition concludes that 'there is very little reason to assume that, while comprehensive schools retain any form of selection through streaming, their effects on talent development will differ from those of tripartite schools' (p.28).

The overall conclusion is that in the change from tripartitism to comprehensive secondary education no fundamental change in the relationship between the educational structure and the occupational structure has been effected. It is worthwhile to quote at length (p.134).

> It has often been noted that while the separate schools of the tripartite system continue to 'feed' different occupational levels one cannot hope for 'parity of esteem' and, given the political priorities of most administrations, parity of material conditions is very unlikely. Yet it is perhaps not generally realised that this

remains true under a 'comprehensive system'. For while the different academic streams are 'feeding' different occupational rivers, prestige and resources will be diverted accordingly.

The work done by Ford comes as a very serious warning especially to those who are interested in furthering socialist objectives on the educational front of the class struggle. There is no magic way to the achievement of the goal of secondary education for all. By itself reorganisation on comprehensive lines will not, it has been shown, result in comprehensive education. And this is because monopoly capitalism with its increasing concentration of capital, the demands upon education on the part of its technology, and the changes begotten by it on the occupational structure of the working class as a whole, must seek to make state education, tripartite or comprehensive, an educational-occupational selection system.

However, no Marxist would expect a change only in the organisation of secondary education to bring about an immediate change in the entirety of educational practice. We may return here to a fundamental proposition of organisation theory which we have found useful in developing a Marxist perspective. This is that the founding of any organisation always, in the first place, realises a reorganisation of ongoing elements. It was therefore to be inevitable that in comprehensive schools there would be pursued for some time to come, the very goals previously pursued in the tripartite system. To expect something else would be to expect a rapid transformation of capitalism and of the social context it generates, of the schools, of the character of the entire teaching force, of orientations in primary schools and of the socially conditioned goals of the children who come to them. That is to say, to expect what appears to be expected by some critics of the comprehensive school, is to expect that the mere reorganisation of secondary education would usher in a social revolution.

But if comprehensive reorganisation will not by itself serve the central aim of the working class in education—abolition of educational-occupational selection—does this make it irrelevant? Certainly not. A tripartite structure cannot but be a selective system and its retention cannot but perpetuate selection. Organisation on comprehensive lines need not involve streaming—either within the comprehensive schools themselves or in the primary schools when children enter them. Again our fundamental organisation theory helps us; the goals pursued in an organisation need not be permanently

N

associated with it; they may give way to other goals. It comes to this: without the end of tripartitism in secondary education the capitalist sponsored allocative rationing of educational resources cannot be challenged over time; with comprehensive secondary education the organisational setting for its annihilation is brought into being. This is not a matter of whether, for propaganda purposes, it is less or 'more difficult to determine how much is spent on whom' (Ford, 1969, p.135). It is a matter of how those forces whose interest it is to bring about the universalistic goal of a well-educated population can gather the strength and the ability to do so.

The aims defined in the last paragraph involve also the discarding of certain notions. One of these is the dogma that 'while different academic streams are "feeding" different occupational rivers, prestige and resources will be diverted accordingly' (ibid., p.134). Now this statement is, theoretically at least, not tenable. First, it is entirely possible to equip workshops and classrooms for 'non-academic' streams and to employ a pupil-teacher ratio for them in such a way as to give such pupils the advantage in resources. Second, it is not impossible to cultivate prestige for occupations involving manual skill and practical ability at the expense of occupations higher in the currently accepted occupational hierarchy.

Pressure for a reallocation of resources can itself perhaps be conducive to a reconsideration of streaming as a system. The awakening of awareness as to the learning, planning, concentration, effort and sensitivity involved in many skilled occupations can certainly bring into question the order of rank presently accorded to occupational statuses. And if this is what governs ultimately policies of differential education the way forward is clear enough.

The rationale for the comprehensive school as tested by Ford is not the only one and much of it is based upon illusion. Children's occupational aspiration or the aspirations their parents have for them cannot alter the occupational structure. In as much as sooner or later the jobs to be occupied will have to be the jobs which are there to be occupied, a pattern of aspiration which corresponds with this, social reality has greater validity than one which does not. Indeed, the fostering of high occupational aspiration is at the root of selection in education, at the root of streaming. But what can make a difference to the occupation structure and incidentally to its ranking order is education as such. For, when a progressively better-educated labour force enters the economy, one important element among the forces of production has changed—the labour force itself. This view points to an educational praxis which places the emphasis on the development and application of knowledge about how children learn, and which relegates the spurious motivation of 'a better job'.

A similar illusion is the notion that the social class element in friendship groupings can be expunged because the children go to a school called comprehensive. First, since the school is streamed and the school-class teachers must therefore differentiate one child from another against selective achievement criteria (*vide* Parsons) the stage is set for peer groupings on that basis. Second, the strata are concurrent with the school as socialising forces. Third, especially in their later years at secondary school, occupation prospects—a powerful anticipatory socialising factor—cannot but consolidate the informal peer groupings on the indicated lines.

We need to point out also that a school which succeeds in reducing consciousness of membership of the working class does not act in the interests of that class. It is therefore gratifying to learn that this is not happening at Cherrydale Comprehensive School. We have seen how the capitalist class maintains its public schools for the re-inforcement of capitalist class consciousness and solidarity and that no equivalent institutions exist for working-class consciousness and solidarity. If then this class consciousness and solidarity persist in spite of formal persuasions and policies at school it can only be because institutions—trade unions, political parties, etc.—external to the school are pervasive enough to do their work informally. But there is no reason to abandon by default all attempts to bring such class consciousness to the secondary schools—especially the compre-hensives—in quite formal ways. Three avenues seem to be immedi-ately open: (i) the representation of working-class organisations on governing bodies; (ii) progress in the development of class conscious-ness of teachers—that is, of their perception of themselves as the teaching proletariat; (iii) growth of pupil or school student unions. And the most important element in that class consciousness would seem to be, in respect of education, the awareness that systems of selection, as well as drives for upward social mobility, serve those who wish to use the schools mainly for the provision of a differenti-ated labour force. The alternative, that schools should above all concern themselves with the intellectual, aesthetic, social and physical development of all children is the kernel of working-class expectation from educational provision. These two opposed goals express the relativist particularism of capitalist class consciousness on the one hand and the universalism of proletarian class consciousness on the other. Since however, the latter orientation is also in the particular interest of the working class, we reach the conclusion that in struggling for its own interests the proletariat does represent the interests and well-being of society as a whole.

Chapter 9

Marxist universalism

Two warnings

It is possible to draw from elements of the foregoing chapters the main lines of a Marxist perspective for education. To do that, however, two possible misunderstandings must be dealt with.

First there is the frequent use of quotations from Marx and Engels. It should not be imagined that only their ideas count. There is a vast literature, and a history of action, even more vast, representing the scientific theoretical aspect of the impulse to world socialism. That this science should be called Marxism is a tribute to the great genius of Karl Marx. And that there is, currently, a renewal of interest in Marxism indicates the renewed force of that impulse. To work out a Marxist strategy in education, therefore, requires not only a study of Marx and Engels and their followers, but demands also the closest consideration of education as part of modern social history.

Then there is the phrase 'dictatorship of the proletariat'. Dictatorship is generally understood to be the opposite of democracy. Yet it is a commonplace to remark that, with or without formally democratic institutions, capitalist class power dictates in a capitalist society. The substitution of working-class power for that brief period when socialist institutions have not matured, is the dictatorship of the proletariat. Whether that power uses parliament or some other instruments of government depends entirely on the circumstances in which it comes into effect. But this dictatorship means nothing else than the imposition of the will of the working class where still there is some other will to the contrary.

The definition of that will requires the widest, most direct participation of members and organisations of the working class. Thus working-class power brings into being a democracy more complete than has so far been experienced since the advent of class society. For education it means that the teachers first and foremost have a responsibility, much greater than before, to be shared with parents, with fellow-workers and with their pupils. The essential direction of that responsibility is towards socialism and thence towards a classless, stateless communist society. Its content is the preparation of today's children for their adequate participation in that history.

If this is the promise held out by Marxist theory what is the reality? How does the history of action measure against the literary expression of scientific socialist theory? After half a century of power to put theory into practice what contribution has the Soviet Union to offer in the way of solutions to educational problems?

Capitalism's educational hopes

Before making that sketch we should briefly glance at capitalism's educational hopes and problems. In this matter we should note a tendency on the part of British sociologists in education to turn often to the USA for ideas and for experience. This is quite natural. The terms of reference in both countries are the same: solve the most pressing educational problems within the structure of capitalist relationships.

No one has outlined the educational ideal of capitalism better than J. B. Conant in *Education in a Divided World* (1948). Here democracy in the American tradition is defined as (i) government based on free elections; (ii) a complex of relatively independent towns and states, etc. in a Federal unity; (iii) a high degree of bureaucratic honesty; (iv) a stratified, highly competitive economic system. The complementarity of educational institutions with this social structure is seen in (v) increasing social mobility and decreasing social distinction, and (vi) increasing equality of opportunity for succeeding generations.

Eighteen years later the American Coleman Report (1966) found that achievements in verbal skills at the age of six varied in accordance with ethnic and regional differences and that twelve years of schooling left them even further apart at the age of eighteen. Halsey points out that 'the rational goal of equality of opportunity, would, if realised, produce converging as opposed to diverging lines' (1973, p.9). Capitalism in America remains strong. America is the richest country in the world. Yet American educationalists have to turn their attention to 'the culture of poverty' in their towns. Nowhere is that culture more evident than in education and nothing gives that culture more support than an educational system geared to meeting the demands of its stratification system.

The situation is not different in Britain where the class and status structure is manifested in the existence of schools which require the help of positive discrimination. Here, as Halsey summarises the progress of the definition of equality of opportunity, we have moved from a self-confessed class orientation of educational institutions through an arrangement boasting equality of access, via an attempt at equality of outcome (as measured by successive redistribution of children among the hierarchy of occupations), to an admission of failure on both counts. The latest redefinition proposes to foster a multi-variant educational system to match a multi-variant society. Since the variety is a stratification system meeting capitalist requirements, this perspective in effect represents a return to an openly ascriptive educational system in line with these requirements. That it will not succeed is ensured by the technological factors in continuous antagonism with current class relationships, and by the universalistic educational aims of the working-class movement.

The Soviet perspective

It is universalism in education which characterises the perspectives at work in the Soviet Union. From the first Soviet education has been avowedly oriented to the promotion of the communist ideal. It has not departed from that stand. In 1946 the activities of teachers were defined by Kairov as (quoted in Hans, 1967, p.210)

(a) care and supervision of the development of the rising generation; (b) the arming of it with systematic knowledge, skill and habits necessary for its future practical activities; and (c) the training of it in the necessary emotions, inclinations, and interests, habits of behaviour, features of will power and character in accordance with the spirit and principles of communist morality.

That communist morality is essentially a universalistic one (ibid., p.211).

The communist ideal . . . is based on the principle of the brotherhood of all peoples, irrespective of their race, creed, language, nation or sex, and is aimed at the liberation of all oppressed groups from economic exploitation or national and racial subjugation.

Universalism in Soviet educational practice has included a policy promoting educational equality among the Union's many nationalities. The national language of each of the republics and of many of the autonomous regions—involving as many as 180 languages—has been the official vehicle of instruction. This policy, elaborated within ten years of the revolution, has achieved mass literacy throughout the Soviet Union. And the compulsory study of Russian where this is not the indigenous language has opened up the Union's cultural heritage to every participating nation (see Hans, ibid., pp.55–8).

Universalism is realised also in those aspects of Soviet educational practice which are of interest to progressive teachers in capitalist countries. Mental testing was widely practised in Britain before and after the Second World War. Only during the 1950s was there the beginning of a revolt against intelligence quotient ideology, and selection at eleven plus. In this British Marxists played their part but it must be admitted that the major factor in the success of this revolt was not an ideological one. It was rather the pressure of technological change. But testing was eliminated from Soviet schools as early as 1936, and a deliberate turn made to the study instead, of the learning process and of ways of facilitating it (see Simon, 1971). What motivates this perspective, however, is that a socialist society requires a highly educated population, that there is no section of society which can profit from illiteracy, or from ignorance, and that the basic phylogenetic characteristic peculiar to human species being is his learning activity. The result is that non-Marxists have seen fit to take the Russian experience as proof that except for a tiny minority all children can learn to use their minds.

The institution of secondary education in common schools with no streaming or tracking, and with a common curriculum takes the universalistic approach further. We are entitled to see in this a deliberate norm of orientation to a future in which divisions between mental and physical labour will cease to have meaning. In terms of Halsey's classification of theories explaining poverty (1972, pp.13–20) neither cultural nor situational complexes are likely to withstand for long the social consciousness and the socialist policies at work in the Soviet Union.

The mode of work of this consciousness and of these policies has been examined by U. Bronfenbrenner, in his comparison of Russian with American child upbringing. The problem of the line joining teacher to parent in the teacher-child-parent triangle is overcome. Moreover it is overcome in such a manner as to obtain not merely the co-operation of the individual child, but that of the peer group as well.

Most significant of all is the Soviet understanding of the role of the teacher and of the function of the school, as role and function excluding selection. But then there is no labour market in the capitalist sense of the term. Socialism has a network of occupations whose requirements must be met; capitalism has a 'structure of opportunities for jobs' (ibid., p.19). The former makes it desirable to strive for everyone to be an educated person; the latter makes desirable a differentiated educational system and imposes rejection for those surplus to the 'opportunities'. Given the rate and direction of development in the forces of production, the socialist educational contribution to co-operative endeavour yields a harmony between relations and forces of production. But with the same technological dynamic, for capitalism jobs are opportunities seized by the most well-equipped competitors and education is training for the competition. The results are periodic crises in the matter of adequately educated manpower, widespread disappointment with the prizes, and a continuous generation of cultural and situational poverty for the rejected and for the non-runners. We have here just one other facet of the antagonism between forces and relations of production with evidence that socialism negates this antagonism.

Besides the outcome of deliberations with regard to intelligence testing, school organisation, curriculum, and social context of the school, there is another credit to be given to Soviet educational endeavour. This is the work on language and thought, work that is completely in line with the now established educational tradition of finding out about how children learn. It is significant that some of our best thinkers in education should acknowledge the Russians in this, whereas the failure of compensatory education under capitalism should produce a resurgence of intelligence testing ideology with Jensen and Eysenck.

The Chinese perspective

The indications from China point in the same direction. Ascriptive

O

processes appropriate to a feudal system of exploitation were only slightly breached by the superimposition of imperialist demands for shares in the surplus product. Indeed since the yield had to increase the exploitation had to be more severe. But where the dominant classes escalated their demands, the producers found impossible the old ways of life. History had brought to the productive forces of China a band of capitalist powers, in rivalry, each against the rest, for the privilege of fastening upon its millions the fetters of capitalist productive relationships.

The millions of peasants and artisans, as well as the more modern proletariat of China, had no literacy. Their education was in the tradition and work of their forebears by custom and example. Letters and intellectual endeavour were requirements mainly from those who served in government. Until 1904 China knew only a centuries-old highly refined examination system which, from a tiny group of competitors, brought scholars into government. Thereafter, until 1949, the beginnings of a school system were strongly influenced by American ideas.

The chasm between the civil servants and the masses was preserved by a system of writing which was not phonetic. Chinese ideographic writing, transcending a variety of dialects and tongues facilitated a central administration. At the same time it made a cultural heritage and democratic participation inaccessible to the vast majority (see Hans, 1961).

But capitalism in its subjugation of China could not fail to bring with it news of a revolutionary proletariat and its theory. If, therefore, the Chinese masses found both feudalism and capitalism impossible modes of social existence, they could take up only a vision of a future that was both practical and in advance of a technically superior civilisation. This vision they found in the theory and practice of Marxism.

The direction of the educational thrust in China is universalist in the first place, therefore, because it openly serves the purpose of building socialism and declares an identity of interest with workers throughout the world. The so-called 'mass line' is another aspect of universalism, for in this it is asserted that an entire people can understand what has to be done and that the major problem is one of facilitating that understanding.

The drive to mass literacy has been of primary importance in this. Dialects and ideographic characters were major obstacles. But a threefold strategy has been developed to overcome them: (i) a policy to universalise Mandarin pronunciation is facilitated by using a phonetic system comprising the twenty-six letters of the Latin alphabet; (ii) a standard simplified use of Chinese characters has been made compulsory for all publications since 1956; (iii) all reading primers use the phonic alphabet as a guide to Mandarin pronunciation of the simplified characters and in achieving readiness to read the characters. (An illustrated account of the process is given by Price, *Education in Communist China*, 1970, p.119.)

Early socialising agencies promote development of a classless society. Since the establishment of the People's Republic, nurseries for children aged one to four have flourished in factories, communes, urban neighbourhoods and mines. The ethical orientations governing their upbringing are characterised by 'a genuine atmosphere of respect for the personal dignity and rights of the child in People's China which is a joy for any educator and humanitarian to see' (Tsang, 1968, p.164), and an infancy in which 'they are brought up to the feeling that they are part of the great society and have their share in its assets and its well-being'.

After the nurseries, kindergartens abound for children from four to seven years. It is notable that in contrast with Taiwan and Hong Kong competitive academic study is absent from kindergartens of the Republic. Here, games, handwork, singing, stories and group activities make up the programme whilst language ability is developed in speech.

The primary schools from seven to thirteen carry forward the same spirit. A common programme is engaged in by all children. From seven to eleven the major emphases are on language and mathematics; from eleven to thirteen nature study, history, geography and physical education complicate the curriculum. What is of primary importance to our theme however, is the absence of individual competition. 'Life in the school is a happy experience . . . the spirit of co-operation and comradeship is seen in every aspect of school life' (ibid., pp.168–9). At the same time appreciation of ordinary work is fostered by the children's participation in labour: cleaning their school and their neighbourhood; working in factories; serving drinking water at tram stops; engaging in social campaigns and so on. It becomes clear that education is not to be thought of as something that raises its possessor to a superior status in life.

The deliberate aim of abolishing the division between mental and manual labour is carried forward in the half-work half-study schools and in spare time education. The aims of these kinds of educational activity are to intellectualise the working people and to cultivate in intellectuals labour habits and attitudes. The extent of the growth of the spare time movement is given by P. Harper as follows: 1949— 276,432; 1951—2,026,381; 1953—2,587,967; 1957—10,000,000; 1960 (February)—19,000,000; 1960 (August)—25,000,000 (quoted in Price, 1970, p.197). Schools for part-time study are set up by factories big enough to do so, or by a group of factories. They are also attached to full-time schools and to communes.

It is not the case, as Hutchins, for example, in *The Learning Society*, seems to think, that the purpose of the educational drive in China is confined to production aims. As Price reports, it is explicitly stated by communist officials that without education the poor and lower peasantry would also be without political power.

It is in this light that the Cultural Revolution should be considered. The most favourable conditions for the growth of élitism are those where, as in China, capital resources for the development of educational institutions are slender. In such conditions family background must count enormously in the fitting of children for graduation from secondary education to higher education. And this is supported by the figures for the percentage of children from worker or peasant families going to universities and comparable organisations. A growth of this proportion from 20·46 per cent in 1952 to nearly 50 per cent in 1965 may be regarded as a rapid transformation. But it would appear from the evidence (see Price, 1970, p.169) that developments have slowed somewhat since 1958. If the Cultural Revolution has cleared away an accumulation of obstacles to the democratisation of power and of education then it has carried forward the surge towards a classless society.

The Chinese revolution is young yet and its education system should not be regarded as having taken permanent shape. We can be sure, however, from the practice of twenty-four years, that Marxism in China inspires educational policies that lift the minds of hundreds of millions to levels of perception and action not dreamed of in countries with similar levels of development but without the same guidance. These policies are part of a revolution in which a transfer of political power and economic betterment are only the first moves in the transformation of every norm of social life. They are part of the process of social revolution.

Education for a classless society

No doubt the social revolution as it unfolds in Russia and China will bring about more successes in education as in other branches of human activity. In addition there will be lessons to be learnt from the other socialist states. But it is unlikely that a completely communist society can be accomplished without socialism in many other countries—including present-day industrially advanced capitalist countries. In this sense too the Marxist perspective is universalistic. For this perspective envisages a world movement, socialism with international dimensions.

We learn from the examples of Russia and China that educational supports for a classless society are possible providing the will to construct them is effective. From a comparison of socialist with capitalist social systems it appears that this effectiveness depends upon the location of political power. Only where the working class is firmly in control does education begin to serve society in general. This is because the major overall difference between the two social systems in respect of child upbringing is whether children are educated or graded. In Britain, therefore, not only the present, but also the ultimate interests of the proletariat are best served by those who wish to make of the schools places where children learn—not institutions of selection and rejection.

Relativism is the sociological standpoint that sees no progress from capitalism and underestimates the force of its contradictions. Particularism is the form of consciousness at group level that can go no further than the immediate, recurring group interests within capitalism's framework. Relativism then is the ideological expression of particularism.

But for every period in history there is a group whose particular interests in the long term correspond with what must be done if the total cultural development is to be taken forward. In other words, there are particular interests which merge with society's universal requirements. Marxism shows that the political and social demands of the modern proletariat represent, at the same time, solutions to the problems of society taken as a whole. This is nowhere clearer than in that area of social activity we call 'education'.

Against the particularism of capitalist interests, therefore, and against its relativist ideology, stands Marxist universalism. This view acknowledges the phenomenon of progress, recognises the unity of human kind, greets the prospect of a classless society, and invites the adventure of its inauguration. When the depth and spread of social revolution is borne in mind it will be seen that a vital source of its power is education. It was for this reason that as early as 1848 Marx and Engels pointed to the need to 'rescue education from the bourgeoisie'.

Select bibliography

ALBROW, M. (1965), 'The study of organizations' in Gould, ed. (1965).

ANDERSON, M., ed. (1971), *The Sociology of the Family*, Penguin, Harmondsworth.

AZCARETE, M. (1973), 'The network of science', *Marxism Today*, March.

BARON, G. (1966), *Society, Schools and Progress in England*, Pergamon, Oxford.

BENEDICT, R. (1971 edn), *Patterns of Culture*, Routledge & Kegan Paul, London.

BENN, C. and SIMON, B. (1970), *Half-Way There*, McGraw-Hill, London.

BERGER, P. and LUCKMANN, T. (1967), *The Social Construction of Reality*, Allan Lane, London.

BERLIN, I. (1963), *Karl Marx*, Oxford University Press, London.

BERNSTEIN, B. (1965), 'A socio-linguistic approach to social learning' in Gould, ed. (1965).

BERNSTEIN, B. (1967), 'Open schools, open society', *New Society*, 14 September.

BERNSTEIN, B. (1971), *Class, Codes and Control*, vol. 1, Routledge & Kegan Paul, London.

BERNSTEIN, B. (1972), 'Education cannot compensate for society' in Rubinstein and Stoneman, eds (1972).

BOHANNAN, P. (1963), *Social Anthropology*, Holt, Rinehart & Winston, New York.

BOTTOMORE, T. (1964), *Elites and Society*, Watts, London.

BRONFENBRENNER, U. (1972), *Two Worlds of Childhood*, Allen & Unwin, London.

BYRNE, D. S. and WILLIAMSON, W. (1971), *The Myth of the Restricted Code*, Working Papers in Sociology No.2, University of Durham.

CASSIRER, E. (1970 edn), *An Essay on Man*, Bantam Books, New York.

CLARKE, F. (1948), *Freedom in the Educative Society*, University of London Press.

COATES, K. and SILBURN, (1972), 'Education in poverty' in Rubinstein and Stoneman, eds (1972).

COLEMAN, J. S. *et al.* (1966), *Equality of Educational Opportunity*, Government Printing Office, Washington.

CONANT, J. B. (1948), *Education in a Divided World*, Harvard University Press, Cambridge, Mass.

COTGROVE, S. S. (1958), *Technical Education and Social Change*, Allen & Unwin, London.

DE CECCO, J. P. (1966), *The Psychology of Language, Thought and Instruction*, Holt, Rinehart & Winston, New York.

DES (1938), *Secondary Education, with special reference to Grammar Schools and Technical High Schools* (Spens Report), HMSO, London.

DES (1943), *Curriculum and Examinations in Secondary Schools* (Norwood Report), HMSO, London.

DES (1946), *Scientific Manpower* (Barlow Report), HMSO, London, Cmnd 6824.

DES (1954), *Early Leaving*, HMSO, London.

DES (1959), *Fifteen to Eighteen* (Crowther Report), HMSO, London.

DES (1963a), *Half our Future*, (Newsom Report), HMSO, London.

DES (1963b), *Higher Education* (Robbins Report), HMSO, London, Cmnd 5174.

DES (1966), *Children and their Primary Schools* (Plowden Report), HMSO, London.

DES (1972), *Education: Framework for Expansion*, HMSO, London, Cmnd 5174.

DEPARTMENT OF TRADE AND INDUSTRY (1968), *The Flow into Employment of Scientists, Engineers and Technologists* (Swann Report), HMSO, London.

DOUGLAS, J. W. B. (1967), *The Home and the School*, Pan, London.

DURKHEIM, ÉMILE (1947 edn), *The Division of Labour in Society*, Free Press, Chicago.

DURKHEIM, ÉMILE (1956 edn), *Education and Sociology*, Free Press, Chicago.

DUTT, R. P. (1953), *The Crisis of Britain and the British Empire*, Lawrence & Wishart, London.

ENGELS, FRIEDRICH (1955 edn), *Anti-Duhring*, Lawrence & Wishart, London.

ENGELS, FRIEDRICH (1956 edn), *On Historical Materialism*, Lawrence & Wishart, London.

ENGELS, FRIEDRICH and MARX, KARL (1958 edn), *On Religion*, Lawrence & Wishart, London.

ENGELS, FRIEDRICH (1972 edn), *Origin of the Family, Private Property and the State*, Lawrence & Wishart, London.

ERIKSON, E. (1964), *Childhood and Society*, Penguin, Harmondsworth.

FLETCHER, R. (1962), *Family and Marriage in Britain*, Penguin, Harmondsworth.

FORD, J. (1969), *Social Class and the Comprehensive School*, Routledge & Kegan Paul, London.

FRIED, M. H. (1960), 'On the evolution of social stratification and the State' in S. Diamond, ed. (1960), *Culture in History*, Columbia University Press, New York.

GERTH, H and MILLS, C. WRIGHT, eds (1948), *From Max Weber*, Routledge & Kegan Paul, London.

GLENNERSTER, H. and PRYKE, J. (1964), *The Public Schools*, Fabian Society, London.

GOULD, J., ed. (1965), *Penguin Survey of the Social Sciences*, Penguin, Harmondsworth.

GOULDNER, A. W. (1970), *The Coming Crisis of Western Sociology*, Heinemann, London.

GRANT, N. (1965), *Soviet Education*, University of London Press.

HALSEY, A. H. (1972), *Educational Priority*, HMSO, London.

HALSEY, A. H., FLOUD, J. and ANDERSON, A. C., eds (1961), *Education, Economy and Society*, Free Press, Chicago.

HANS, N. (1967), *Comparative Education*, Routledge & Kegan Paul, London.

HENRY, J. (1971), *Essays in Education*, Penguin Harmondsworth.

HOMANS, G. (1951), *The Human Group*, Routledge & Kegan Paul, London.

HOPPER, E., ed. (1971), *Readings in the Theory of Educational Systems*, Hutchinson, London.

HUTCHINS, R. M. (1970), *The Learning Society*, Penguin, Harmondsworth.

KALTON, G. (1966), *The Public Schools*, Longman, London.

KOGAN, M., ed. (1971), *The Politics of Education*, Penguin, Harmondsworth.

KRADER, L. (1968), *Formation of the State*, Prentice Hall, Englewood Cliffs.

LAMBERT, R. *et al.* (1970), *A Manual to the Sociology of the School*, Weidenfeld & Nicolson, London.

LANE, T. and ROBERTS, K. (1971), *Strike at Pilkingtons*, Fontana, London.

LÉVI-STRAUSS, C. (1968), *Elementary Structures of Kinship*, Eyre & Spottiswoode, London.

LINTON, R. (1947), *Cultural Background of Personality*, Routledge & Kegan Paul, London.

LOUNSBURY, F. L. (1970), 'Language and culture' in S. Hook, ed. (1970), *Language and Philosophy*, University of London Press.

LURIA, A. R. (1961), *The Role of Speech in the Regulation of Normal and Abnormal Behaviour*, Pergamon, Oxford.

LURIA, A. R. and YUDOVITCH, F. I. (1971), *Speech and the Development of the Mental Processes in the Child*, Penguin, Harmondsworth.

MACLURE, S. (1965), *Educational Documents in England and Wales 1816–1963*, Chapman & Hall, London.

MARSH, D. C. (1968), *The Changing Social Structure of England and Wales*, Routledge & Kegan Paul, London.

MARX, KARL (1918 edn), *Introduction to a Critique of Political Economy*, Kerr, London.

MARX, KARL, (1926 edn), *Capital*, vols I, II, III, Lawrence & Wishart, London.

MARX, KARL and ENGELS, FRIEDRICH (1948 edn), *The Communist Manifesto* Lawrence & Wishart, London.

MARX, KARL and ENGELS, FRIEDRICH (1958 edn), *On Religion*, Lawrence & Wishart, London.

MARX, KARL and ENGELS, FRIEDRICH (1965 edn), *The German Ideology*, Lawrence & Wishart, London.

MARX, KARL and ENGELS, FRIEDRICH (1968 edn), *Selected Works*, vols I and II, Lawrence & Wishart, London.

MARX, KARL and ENGELS, FRIEDRICH (1969 edn), *Basic Writings on Philosophy and Politics*, ed. L. Feuer, Fontana, London.

MIDWINTER, E. (1972), *Priority Education*, Penguin, Harmondsworth.

MINISTRY OF LABOUR (1964), *Manpower Studies No. 1*, HMSO, London.

MINISTRY OF LABOUR (1965), *Manpower Studies No. 2*, HMSO, London.

MUSGRAVE, P. W. (1965), *Sociology of Education*, Methuen, London.

MUSGRAVE, P. W. (1968a), *The School as an Organization*, Macmillan, London.

MUSGRAVE, P. W. (1968b), *Society and Education in England since 1800*, Methuen, London.

NEWSOM, J. and NEWSOM, E. (1966), *Patterns of Infant Care in an Urban Community*, Penguin, Harmondsworth.

NEWSOM, J. and NEWSOM, E. (1968), *Four Years Old in an Urban Community*, Allen & Unwin, London.

PARSONS, T. (1951), *The Social System*, Routledge & Kegan Paul, London.

PARSONS, T. (1961), 'The school class as a social system' in Halsey, Floud and Anderson, eds (1961).

PARSONS, T. and BALES, R. F. (1956), *Family, Socialisation and Interaction Process*, Routledge & Kegan Paul, London.

PETRAS, J. W. and CURTIS, J. E., eds (1970), *The Sociology of Knowledge: Readings*, Duckworth, London.

PRICE, R. F. (1970), *Education in Communist China*, Routledge & Kegan Paul, London.

RAPOPORT, R. and RAPOPORT, R. N. (1971), 'Family roles and work roles' in Anderson, ed. (1971).

REX, J. (1961), *Key Problems in Sociological Theory*, Routledge & Kegan Paul, London.

RUBINSTEIN, D. and SIMON, B. (1969), *Evolution of the Comprehensive School*, Routledge & Kegan Paul, London.

RUBINSTEIN, D. and STONEMAN, C. eds, (1972), *Education for Democracy*, Penguin, Harmondsworth.

SAHLINS, M. (1968), *Tribesmen*, Prentice Hall, Englewood, Cliffs.

SAPIR, E. (1962), *Culture, Language and Personality*, University of California Press, Berkeley.

SHIPMAN, M. D. (1968), *The Sociology of the School*, Longman, London.

SHIPMAN, M. D. (1971), *Education and Modernisation*, Faber, London.

SIMON, B. (1965), *Education and the Labour Movement*, Lawrence & Wishart, London.

SIMON, B. (1971), *Intelligence, Psychology and Education*, Lawrence & Wishart, London.

SMITH, ADAM (1970 edn), *Wealth of Nations*, ed. Andrew Skinner, Penguin, Harmondsworth.

SOROKIN, P. (1964 edn), *Social and Cultural Mobility*, Collier-Macmillan, New York.

STALIN, J. (1950), *Concerning Marxism in Linguistics*, Soviet News Booklet.

TIBBLE, J. W., ed. (1966), *The Study of Education*, Routledge & Kegan Paul, London.

TROPP, A. (1957), *The School Teachers*, Heinemann, London.

TSANG, CHIU-SAM (1968), *Society, Schools and Progress in China*, Pergamon, Oxford.

TURNER, R. (1971), 'Modes of social ascent through education', in Hopper, ed. (1971).

VYGOTSKY, L. (1962), *Thought and Language*, MIT Press, Cambridge, Mass.

WAKEFORD, J. (1969), *The Cloistered Elite*, Macmillan, London.

WILLIAMS, R. (1961), *The Long Revolution*, Penguin, Harmondsworth.

WILLMOT, P. and YOUNG, M. (1957), *Family and Kinship in East London*, Routledge & Kegan Paul, London.

Index

750   750
120   .25
      3750
     1500
     187,50
600   56

46.6
2 560
  490
  800
  2
807 - 810